Learning in the Lifelong Learning Sector

Also available from Continuum

Learning to Teach in the Lifelong Learning Sector

Ewan Ingleby, Dawn Joyce and Sharon Powell

A companion website to accompany this book is available online
at: http://education.ingleby.continuumbooks.com

Please visit the link and register with us to receive your password and to access these downloadable
resources.

If you experience any problems accessing the resources, please contact Continuum
at: info@continuumbooks.com

continuum

Continuum International Publishing Group

The Tower Building   80 Maiden Lane
11 York Road   Suite 704, New York
London SE1 7NX   NY 10038

www.continuumbooks.com

British Library Cataloguing-in-Publication Data
A catalogue record for this book is available from the British Library.

ISBN: 978-1-4411-8296-8 (paperback)

Library of Congress Cataloging-in-Publication Data
A catalog record for this book is available from the Library of Congress.

Typeset by Newgen Imaging Systems Pvt Ltd, Chennai, India
Printed and bound in India by Replika Press Pvt Ltd

Contents

Introduction

This book is about learning to teach in the Lifelong Learning Sector. Ingleby and Hunt (2008) make reference to the sector being characterized by a range of educational institutions offering an even more varied range of educational programmes. This means that the Lifelong Learning Sector is characterized by diversity, with complex educational challenges presenting a range of fascinating issues for teachers and learners to consider. It can be as Geertz (1998: 2) has phrased 'Heraclitus cubed and worse'! The state of flux that has been popularized by the philosopher Heraclitus is made manifest within the institutions that make up the Lifelong Learning Sector. There are large-scale 'mixed-economy' institutions offering 'higher education' and 'further education'. Alongside this form of provision, there are small-scale institutions offering either 'higher education' or 'further education'. Many of these educational institutions have their origins in the postwar educational expansion of the 1950s and 1960s. Many colleges are also characterized by the reported 'state-of-the-art' learning and teaching facilities that have resulted from New Labour's 'Private Finance Initiative' (PFI) policy of building new or refurbished Lifelong Learning centres.

The learners who are educated in these institutions are also characterized by diversity. There are school pupils studying vocational subjects such as 'health and social care' alongside adults studying degree-level qualifications such as the 'Early Years Sector Endorsed Foundation Degree'. Moreover, the staff working in this environment are also from a range of backgrounds. There are academics with Ph.D. qualifications, teachers with Qualified Teacher

Status (QTS), and lecturers with vocational backgrounds in areas such as 'painting and decorating' who may not have any formal teaching qualifications.

Anyone teaching in the Lifelong Learning Sector needs to learn how to teach. It can be suggested that the process is based on learning, experience and reflective practice. This book engages with the fascinating processes that characterize the Lifelong Learning Sector.

Book structure

The book's six main chapters are based on academic modules that contribute to the Teesside University's Qualified Teacher Learning and Skills Post Graduate Certificate in Education (QTLS PGCE). The book is useful for anyone teaching in the Lifelong Learning Sector. Within the book, there are formative activities that consider practical learning and teaching issues alongside an academic analysis of pedagogy. This provides the opportunity for reflective practice within the Lifelong Learning Sector.

An important theme of the book is to emphasize the link between theory, practice, reflection and learning about teaching. This means that the theoretical concepts are considered to be most useful when they are applied to particular Lifelong Learning contexts. All of the chapters in the book contain formative activities that aim to apply teaching and learning themes to particular Lifelong Learning contexts. These activities engage the reader with the idea that learning about teaching in the Lifelong Learning Sector never ends.

The book's chapters focus upon six main themes:

- preparing to teach in the Lifelong Learning Sector,
- teaching in the Learning and Skills Sector,
- theories and principles for planning and enabling learning and assessment,
- classroom management,
- curriculum development for inclusive practice, and
- research methods for the Lifelong Learning Sector.

Chapter 1 considers 'pre-service' issues within the Lifelong Learning Sector. The chapter provides an introduction to teaching and discusses the basics of planning and preparation for teaching and learning. The chapter explores key 'pre-service' themes, such as 'lesson planning' and 'resource design', in relation to preparing to teach in the Lifelong Learning Sector.

Chapter 2 explores teaching and learning in a variety of educational contexts. The chapter provides an introduction to the key Lifelong Learning theme of 'personal action planning'. The chapter also reviews teaching and learning theories (such as behaviourism, humanism and constructivism) alongside exploring central themes in the Lifelong Learning Sector, such as 'forms of assessment' and 'reflective practice'. The chapter acknowledges that a variety of learners are present within the Lifelong Learning Sector. This necessitates knowledge of a range of teaching and learning strategies.

Chapter 3 considers the theories and principles that inform teaching in relation to planning and enabling learning and assessment. The chapter reviews theories and principles of learning, assessment and communication. The chapter explores how these theories and principles can be used to enable inclusive learning. The final section of the chapter discusses how teaching and assessment can be developed by applying 'theories of learning' to 'reflection on practice'.

Chapter 4 applies the psychological perspectives of behaviourism, humanism and biological, psychodynamic and cognitive theory to 'classroom management'. These perspectives are related to classroom management via case-study examples and formative activities. The chapter ends by assessing the merits of each of the perspectives in respect of the contribution being made to classroom management.

Chapter 5 considers the different educational contexts of the Lifelong Learning Sector. The chapter reflects on 'inclusive practice'. A key theme of this chapter is the exploration of 'inclusive practice' in relation to planning, implementing and evaluating programmes of learning. The chapter considers issues associated with 'inclusion'. The chapter addresses some of the issues that are associated with planning, designing, implementing and reviewing a curriculum that promotes 'inclusive practice'.

Chapter 6 discusses key research perspectives and key research methods that are used within the Lifelong Learning Sector. The chapter begins by identifying the research process. It then identifies the origins of key research paradigms, such as normative, interpretive and action research perspectives. The chapter considers methodological strategies employed by qualitative and quantitative research in relation to lifelong learning. The chapter ends by discussing the relative merits of these research paradigms and methods by reflecting on the value of the research process for the Lifelong Learning Sector

The book provides a comprehensive coverage of key themes impacting on the Lifelong Learning Sector. As opposed to being a general teacher education textbook, it is specifically written for the Lifelong Learning teacher education programmes based on the QTLS standards. This means that the book combines practical experience alongside sound academic analysis.

Learning features

The book stimulates learning through interactive activities within each chapter. As well as these activities, there are case studies and research tasks. The book develops analytical skills through a creative engagement with the content. Alongside the interactive learning activities, there are supporting references so that learning to teach in the Lifelong Learning Sector can be synthesized in relation to these texts.

Standards for QTLS

Tummons (2007: 23) cites 1st January 2005 as a pivotal time for the Lifelong Learning Sector. This is because this date witnessed the emergence of Lifelong Learning UK (LLUK). LLUK now operates as the body responsible for the professional development of all employees who are working within the Lifelong Learning Sector. Alongside LLUK, a subsidiary organization called Standards Verification UK (SVUK) assumed responsibility for approving and endorsing teacher training qualifications within the post-compulsory sector. This role was once carried out by the Further Education Teaching Organisation (FENTO), the organization that has been replaced by LLUK and SVUK. Moreover, at the same time, the Department for Education and Skills (DFES) introduced a new range of qualifications for teacher training in the post-16 sector. This culminated in the introduction of a new set of occupational standards in 2007. These new standards replaced the FENTO standards in order to emphasize the importance of the sector responding to a broad lifelong learning agenda. The DFES considered that the previous FENTO standards were limited due to their focus on 'further education'. In contrast, 'lifelong learning' is deemed as covering all aspects of post-compulsory learning. This means that the new standards are detailed and comprehensive.

Professional development and reflective practice

A major aim of the PGCE programme at the Teesside University is to nurture professionals who are able to reflect on aspects of best practice. This book facilitates self-analysis in relation to the Lifelong Learning Sector. From this self-reflection there is the possibility of development in relation to meeting the complex needs of teachers and learners working in the sector. In realizing this aim, the book achieves some of the ideals of the current QTLS Standards.

References

Geertz, C. (1998), *After the Fact*. Cambridge, MA: Harvard University Press.

Ingleby, E. and Hunt, J. (2008), 'The CPD needs of mentors in post-compulsory Initial Teacher Training in England', *Journal of In-Service Education*, 34, 61–75.

Tummons, J. (2007), *Becoming a Professional Tutor in the Lifelong Learning Sector*. Exeter, UK: Learning Matters.

Preparing to Teach in the Lifelong Learning Sector

Learning Outcomes

After reading this chapter you should be able to

identify the key characteristics of a good teacher,
prepare simple planning documentation,
create a stimulating learning environment which is motivating and inclusive,
identify specific barriers to learning,
create an individual learning plan,
recognize what is meant by the term 'educare'.

Introduction

Preparing to Teach in the Lifelong Learning Sector (PTLLS) is a relatively new qualification, which is the minimum standard qualification when working in a teaching/training/ education environment.

The qualification consists of the following five key areas:

roles and responsibilities
approaches to teaching and learning
planning sessions
managing the environment and motivating and including learners
assessment and record keeping

Each area relates directly to the role of the teacher (or trainer or instructor). The qualification provides the basic information that is required to be effective as a teacher in order to ensure that learners' needs are recognized and met.

Throughout the chapter, there are formative activities that reinforce learning in relation to the key areas of PTLLS that are of relevance for the Lifelong Learning Sector. The chapter makes links to action planning for personal and academic development. The chapter ends by giving an overview of the implications of the concept 'educare' for the Lifelong Learning Sector. This term refers to the emphasis that is now placed upon organizations that come together and work together in cooperation within the Lifelong Learning Sector.

The role of the teacher

Activity 1.1

What are the skills and qualities of a teacher in the Lifelong Learning Sector?

Feedback

When questioning a group of Postgraduate Certificate in Education students about what they thought the skills and qualities of a good teacher were the group came up with the following ideas:

A clear and up-to-date understanding of the subject being delivered.
Motivating to students, both in the way they deliver the subject and in their own enthusiasm for the topic.
Has a good sense of humour.
Can praise and reward students appropriately.
Has high expectations.

This is interesting when compared with a survey of 11- 12-year-olds who identified their views on skills and qualities of a teacher to be as follows:

⇨

A good teacher is		
Kind Generous Listens to you Likes teaching Encourages you Has faith in you Likes their subject Keeps confidences	Does not give up on you Takes time to explain Allows you to speak Tells you how to improve Helps when you are stuck Cares for your opinion	Makes you feel clever Treats people equally Stands up for you Makes allowances Tells the truth Is forgiving

Quality of teaching and learning

Using the Common Inspection Framework 2009, Office for Standards in Education (OFSTED) inspect providers within the Lifelong Learning Sector follow specific criteria. These criteria include the following statements:

How well do learners achieve and enjoy their learning?
How effectively do teaching, training and assessment support learning and development?
How effectively does self-assessment improve the quality of the provision and outcomes for learners?

During classroom observations, observers are looking for the quality of teaching and learning. Quality of learning can be identified as follows:

What have the students learnt?
What is the overall competence of the students?
What is the attitude to learning shown by the students?

When identifying the attitude shown by the learners, observers are checking the interest and motivation shown by the group as well as how well they stay on task. Do the learners concentrate and work cooperatively with others in the group and with the tutor? These are the aspects which identify the quality of learning. However, the quality of teaching can be demonstrated by the following:

Thorough planning documentation which identifies the learning outcomes to be achieved. (Simple planning documentation will be discussed later in this chapter.)
Learning outcomes are shared with the learners and checked for their achievement. Learners are encouraged to self-assess their own achievement of these outcomes.
Teaching methods chosen are appropriate to the achievement of the outcomes and the needs of the learners.
The overall organization of the session along with the teacher's competence in delivery.

How is the quality of teaching and learning assessed?

Using an 'observation proforma', observers for teacher training awards give feedback on specific areas which meet the overarching professional standards of the awards. The standards are set by Standards Verification UK (SVUK) and are used by all organizations delivering the Preparing to Teach in the Lifelong Learning Sector (PTLLS), Certificate in Teaching in the Lifelong Learning Sector (CTLLS) and Diploma in Teaching in the Lifelong Learning Sector (DTLLS) awards.

Planning

When analysing whether a session is properly planned and prepared, an observer considers the lesson plan, scheme of work and the associated documentation produced by the student teacher. Are the session aims and learning outcomes realistic with differentiation of the student group considered? Planning learning means making decisions concerning the 'who, what, why, when, where and how'.

Who are the learners: What are the different levels of ability, what initial assessments have been carried out and what does this tell you about the individuals in the group?

What to teach: This is the consideration of the topic and could be decided by the order of the text book or curriculum syllabus. You might decide to teach what could be considered the easiest topic first to gain group confidence and familiarity with you as a teacher and a new group of learners. There might be a theme or logical sequence to your topics; in other words, if you are teaching basic numeracy, you would teach addition/subtraction before multiplication and division. Perhaps you are working with National Vocational Qualification (NVQ) students who may have to study a Health and Safety module before moving onto other modules and going out into the workplace.

Why is it being taught: As the tutor for the session, you must have a clear reason for delivering the topic; if you do not see the relevance of the session, neither will your learners. Is this a critical session which links together a number of previous weeks' learning? Or is it the beginning of a new theme? The topic could be revision or portfolio building; either way you must have a clear reason or teacher's aim for its delivery.

When will the session be taught: First lesson on Monday mornings or last lesson on a Friday can be difficult. Knowing your group is the key to planning appropriate activities which will maintain interest and motivation. Lessons straight after a break will also need consideration as students will need to be focused and kept on task.

Where will the teaching take place: Think about the venue, location and room layout. Many new college room designs can be small but accommodate the maximum number of students. Consider how you will be able to move around the classroom to facilitate activities. How will the students be able to move into small/large groups to complete activities set? When thinking about the room, do you know what hard resources will be available to you; for example, will there be computer facilities that will enable you to use PowerPoint or show internet clips? Is there an Interactive White Board or a standard 'wipe board' in the room? Knowing the location and resources available will impact on how you plan activities and how you will organize and manage the session.

How will the teaching be carried out, and how will the learning be tested: This is where you will need to consider the content of the session. We mentioned earlier that it is important to ensure that the focus is on learning. This means that the teaching strategies/methods chosen need to ensure the learning outcomes are met and there is opportunity for you and the learners to assess their achievement.

Good planning and preparation is the key to effective lessons. Documenting all aspects of the lesson in a detailed plan shows that you have given great consideration to all aspect of the lesson from the introduction and main body through to the consolidation and conclusion section.

A simple lesson plan design

There are many lesson plan designs; however, at this stage in your teacher training a simple plan design could look like this:

Lesson plan

Course	Session title		Level(s)		
Day and time	Session number				
Room	Tutor				
Aims of session:					
Objectives (learning outcomes) All learners will be able to 1. 2. 3. 4.			Some learners will be able to 1. 2. A few learners will be able to 1. 2.		
Overview of group:					
Differentiation (identify how you cater for different learning styles, levels of ability and experience, special needs etc)					

Time	Content	Teacher activity (including assessment)	Learner activity	Resources	Additional comments (e.g., Information Learning Technology (ILT), key/basic skills, assessment criteria, differentiation)
	Introduction				
	Development Learning Outcome 1				
	Learning Outcome 2				
	Learning Outcome 3				
	Conclusion				

The above table is a simple format which will start to get you thinking about the important aspects of the lesson. It is shown as a two-section table; the first section is often known as a 'preamble' to the main content section. The preamble details the 'who, what, when and where' were discussed previously. It also shows the overall aim and learning outcomes for the session.

Lesson aims

Aims or educational goals are clear and concise statements that describe what the teacher hopes to achieve. They tend to be broad statements which are expressed from the teacher's perspective or from the course syllabus. Aims may not be fully achieved by the end of a lesson, module or course but could be something that develop over the curriculum. A general lesson aim could be 'to create opportunities for learners to engage in critical reflection'. Petty (1998) states, 'aims are like compass directions, indicating the general direction in which the teacher wishes to travel.' Aims may point you in the right direction, but they do not tell you how to get there. Therefore, you need to have a more detailed description. These learning aims are often referred to as learning outcomes.

Learning outcomes

Learning outcomes are the targets we set for our learners. They must always start with a verb; this helps students to see the action required from them. When you are writing learning outcomes which are knowledge based, it is important to avoid the verb 'understand' because it is difficult to test and measure achievement. Outcomes must clearly identify what you want or intend the students to learn. They must be assessable and measurable to ensure achievement; therefore, the lesson plan must have activities that allow you to assess the outcomes. When writing learning outcomes think of smart target setting; in other words, be specific. It is also important to ensure that the outcomes are measurable, achievable, realistic and 'time-bound'.

Clear, specific, well-written learning outcomes take time to write; however, for the learners this is their guide to achieving the teacher's aim. Take time to practice this skill, and compare your learning outcomes to other experienced teachers working within your department. To assist with writing learning outcomes, it is useful to be aware of the Domains of Learning.

Domains of learning

The way in which we learn depends to a certain extent on the type of learning that is involved. There are three main types (or domains) of learning, and each type has 'rules' associated with it.

Writers tend to separate into three main groups or domains. These are the psychomotor, cognitive and affective domains. This is summarised in Table 1.1:

Table 1.1 Useful verbs for showing learning in each domain

Domain	Possible verbs
Psychomotor	Shows skills in the following: assemble, build, cook, design, fillet, mend, paper, sing, weigh
Cognitive	Know, define, label, list, name, outline, state, interpret, translate, explain, give new examples, summarize
Affective	Appreciate, ask, choose, answer, comply, study, check

Source: Adapted from Reece and Walker (2007: 15).

Those skills that are concerned with physical dexterity (e.g., changing a wheel or giving an injection) fall into the *psychomotor* domain. Both of the tasks do need knowledge, but predominantly, they are physical skills which need practice and depend upon coordination. Knowledge and knowing the 'how' and the 'why' (or the thinking skills) fall into the *cognitive* domain, whereas the skills that deal with feelings and emotions are in the *affective* domain. This means that they are different from the examples in the other learning domains.

Learning in these three domains often needs different teaching and learning approaches. They are often considered in isolation, but in practice learning may occur simultaneously in all three.

Psychomotor: It relates to the measurement of the student's manual skill performances, and therefore, the performance required will involve the manipulation of objects, tools, supplies or equipment. Performances which are primarily psychomotor include the following:

Typing a letter.
Constructing a wall.
Driving a car
Drawing a picture.

Cognitive: It includes those learning behaviours requiring 'thought processes' (in other words, thinking) for specific information, such as 'defines terms', 'select a suitable material' and 'summarize the topic'.
Affective: The behaviour required in this domain involves the demonstration of feelings, emotions or attitudes towards other people, ideas or things. For example, the student might be asked to

demonstrate an increased awareness of environmental pollution,
show concern for safety in the workshop,
display an appropriate attitude towards a frightened patient.

The learning required of the student related to each of the domains is quite different, and indeed the learning in the cognitive domain at the level of knowledge is different from that required for understanding.

Differentiated learning outcomes

Question: What are differentiated learning outcomes?
Answer: Learning outcomes that allow you to set targets for students at different levels.

Think of

- All – what everyone must do to pass.
- Some – what students have to do to achieve 'merit' level.
- Few – what students have to do to achieve 'distinction' level.

The following are some examples in practice:

- In history

  All students will be able to identify the causes of the Peasants' Revolt.
  Some students will be able to explain how each cause led to the revolt.
  A few students may also be able to explain the links between the causes.

- In drama

  All students will be able to produce a mask relevant to the storyline.
  Some students will be able to make a mask appropriate to the genre.
  A Few students may also be able to make a mask that represents their in-depth character study.

Practise writing learning outcomes to accommodate the different levels of learners in your group, but remember all students need to achieve the 'all' learning outcomes as a baseline.

Lesson plan – content section

The main content section describes 'the how'. An effective session consists of the following stages:

An introduction: This 'sets the scene' by reviewing previous learning and making links to the session through stating the learning outcomes to be achieved. It is good practice to show these learning outcomes visually as well as stating them verbally. Some very good teaching sessions have these learning outcomes visible throughout the session where the teacher can refer to their achievement and the learners can self-assess their competence against each one. During this stage of the lesson, use oral questions to initially engage and focus learners of the session topic. An original introduction can play a dramatic role in the session. As a general rule, keep the introduction to a maximum of ten minutes to avoid the wrong response, for example, sending them to sleep!

The development stage or main body of the lesson: This is where all new learning is delivered and applied. The session plan example shows how the learning outcomes could be broken up during this development stage, ensuring each is delivered and assessed. New learning needs to be applied. Therefore ensure that there is sufficient opportunity for learners to complete activities in order to apply their new learning to a given situation. Within this section, it is important to plan assessment opportunities. How will you be able to assess the learners' achievements? Popular strategies include the following: observation of the activities learners are completing, question and answer (Q&A), group work with feedback and small group presentations. As a guide, keep your presentation sections (teacher talk) to a maximum of 20 minutes before moving on to an activity; this keeps the learners focused and ensures a good pace to the session is maintained.

Conclusion: A conclusion section is important to review the learning outcomes and how they have been achieved. Q&A is a good strategy to use during this section of the lesson. Ask the learners to tell you how the outcomes have been met (in other words, what have they done within the session, what were the main outcomes from the activities). Effective lessons ensure that there are opportunities for learners to self-assess their own achievements of the learning outcomes. This is also the section where following the review you make links to the next session.

Each of these sections of the lesson are as important as each other. Without a focused introduction, the learners may be unaware of the expectations and the overall 'big picture'. Too much teacher talk within the development section may leave the students demotivated and uninterested. It is also important to be aware that without a solid roundup of the lesson and links to further learning learners may be unaware of any achievements.

Lesson evaluation

All the above elements are vital components in the session-planning activity of the teacher. However, for a number of reasons, you may not be satisfied the first time around. Experience will show that improvements or modifications may be required. For this reason, it is essential that the teacher evaluates not only the students' attainments but also the way the session has progressed and whether learning actually took place. Evaluation will include elements such as the following:

> The use of discussion at the end of the session, comparing results with the learning outcomes stated for the session.
> Asking, "If I taught this subject again, what changes would I make?"

Your own self-evaluation of what you do as a teacher is critical to your professional development. As a starting point, you could use the checklist below to help you evaluate the plans you produce.

Checklist for the planning of sessions

Are the learning outcomes clearly stated?
Have you ascertained the previous knowledge of the students?
Are all the materials and examples at hand?
Have you selected appropriate teaching methods in relation to the outcomes?
Are the learning activities appropriate to the group?
Is the material sequenced in a logical manner?
How will you evaluate that learning has taken place?
Is the session plan presented clearly so that you can easily use it?
Are the supporting materials and teaching aids completed?
Is the room/workshop identified, and will it be prepared?
Have you timed the session phases appropriately?
Will your teaching and learning activities motivate?
Have you planned for variety and activity?

Finally, following the delivery of the session teachers need to evaluate. Some self-evaluation questions you could ask yourself include the following:

Was I well prepared?
Was I clear and audible?
Was the session aimed at the correct level?
Did I enjoy the session?
Were the learning outcomes achieved?
Was I dressed correctly?
Was I competent and confident?
Did I motivate the learners?
Was there interaction between learners and between tutor and learners?
Did they respond to the session?
What were the most/least effective parts of the lesson?
Did I make any changes during the session?
Was the time well used or wasted?
Was the session a relaxed learning atmosphere?

How do you become a good teacher/trainer?

Teachers are not born and they are not made by their teacher training tutors. We can say that good teachers make themselves. Geoff Petty's (1998) research shows that there are no personality types that particularly make good teachers. You do not have to be an enthusiastic extrovert. To a large extent, we learn to play the role of teacher, and as we practice we feel more confident in that role. We only succeed if we know how to learn from our mistakes and successes. This is revealed by Figure 1.1:

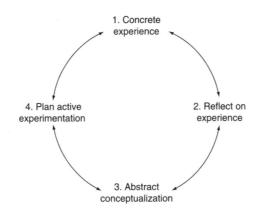

Figure 1.1 Learning from experience (Kolb's learning cycle)

1. Concrete experience is the actual 'doing'.
2. Reflect on experience in order to learn.

> Reflection must be honest and not defensive, which is going to be painful!
> Mistakes are not only inevitable but they are also a necessary part of learning.
> Reflection should not be overcritical.
> Reflection should be carried out honestly, acknowledging both successes and failures.
> *Our business in life is not to succeed, but to continue to fail in good spirits* – Robert Louis Stevenson.

3. Abstract conceptualization refers to asking and answering questions such as the following:

> 'Why didn't that activity work?'
> 'What went wrong at the end of the lesson?'

4. Active experimentation

This can be frightening as it may mean that we tend to develop survival strategies, rather than effective teaching techniques! This means that ideally we should try to take some risks.

Managing self-evaluation. How are you going to evaluate your own teaching?

Here are some suggestions:

> Fill in a self-evaluation form. Use a pro-forma or write more freely about your lesson.
> Ask your students to comment.
> Video your lesson – view and then write a self-evaluation.
> Focus on particular highs or lows in your lesson – comment on what happened and then reflect on the experience.

The aim of self-evaluation is to make you into a 'reflective practitioner' – so that your aim is to constantly improve.

Barriers to learning

Finding out about our learners is an important part of the planning stage and the basis for differentiating between our learners. When looking at the simple lesson plan, we thought about 'who, what, when, where and how'; we now need to research further into 'who'!

Why do we need to know about our learners?

We need to identify any specific barriers to learning, identify special needs, identify particular interests of the group, identify particular likes/dislikes of the group and use the information to effectively plan lessons. In addition, we also need to devise individual learning plans (ILPs).

How do we find out about our learners?

Some of the early methods we use during interview and induction activities could be the use of academic tests, for example, literacy and numeracy assessments. One of the most popular testing methods used within further education colleges is the Basic and Key Skill Builder (BKSB) programme. This programme enables tutors to find out the specific working level of learners using an initial assessment (in other words, entry level up to Level 2 or General Certificate of Secondary Education [GCSE] equivalent). Further use of this programme can identify specific areas of weakness using the diagnostic assessment, that is, spelling, grammar or fractions, area and so on. This early indication of literacy and/or numeracy ability, determined through their way of finding studies, can determine whether learners need additional support. Aptitude testing is also a method used for identifying areas of initial expertise, perhaps in a specific skill area, for example, in vocational programmes. Enrolment forms can also provide the tutor with a wealth of information, including age, gender and ethnicity. It is also important to consider previous qualifications and previous places of study. Pre-course interviews can help in identifying a learner's suitability for a course. This enables the contents of the student's application form to be discussed at greater length. Occasionally students may not meet the official programme entry requirements, but after discussing the person's background and considering their previous experiences there may be the possibility of accessing the programme. These 'exceptional entries' can give a nontraditional route onto the course of study.

Learning styles tests have become a very popular method of finding out about our learners. These tests identify the learners' preferred learning style. Having this information helps us to plan more carefully the activities which will ensure learners learn.

Learning styles and Herrmann's 'whole brain' model

Herrmann developed this model in 1982 for use with adults in business. It is assumed that the model works outside of business studies, and this seems very likely. Hermann identifies four leaning styles related to 'right brain' and 'left brain' styles.

Left brain: theorist and organizer
Right brain: innovator and humanitarian

A review of learning style systems carried out by Frank Coffield rated Herrmann's system as one of the best available (www.lsrc.ac.uk/publications).

As teachers, we need to find out about the learning preferences of our learners, but we need to aim for 'whole brain learning' by using a variety of teaching methods to teach the learning objectives. This means that we need to teach the learning objectives upon considering each learning style. The learning styles are seen as being complementary parts of the whole process as opposed to being alternatives to choose from. This means that teachers should try to help their students to work effectively in all styles, even if this requires students to move beyond their 'comfort zones'.

The work of Herrmann (and Apter, also reviewed positively by Coffield) suggests that learners may gain enormous pleasure if they move between opposite styles, even if they are initially resistant to doing this. Working with opposites helps learners to become more creative and to see their work as more varied and interesting. Herrmann positively encourages change and growth, by getting students to work on their weak styles.

The whole brain model was originally thought to be based on the physiology of the brain, but 'left brain' functions have been found in the right brain and vice versa, so the 'left' and 'right' functions are now thought of as metaphors for different thinking styles and functions.

As with all learning styles systems, there is a danger that users will use the process in order to stereotype. Learners are able to use all styles and should be encouraged to use them all. (Arguably learners with Aspergers syndrome or extreme autism have very strong preference for the left styles and very low functioning for the right.)

Herrmann identifies four learning styles based on a right/left brain approach:

Theorist – the rational self

1. Upper left quadrant A (males often prefer this)

Likes logical, rational and mathematical activities (as opposed to emotional, spiritual, musical, artistic, reading, arts and crafts, introvert or feelings activities).

Learns by acquiring and quantifying facts, applying analysis and logic, thinking through ideas, building cases, forming theories.

Learners respond to formalized lecture; content which includes data, financial/technical case discussions, textbooks and bibliographies; programmed learning; behaviour modification.

Innovators – the experimental self.

2. Upper right quadrant D

> Likes innovating, conceptualising, creating, imaginative, original, artistic activities (as opposed to controlled, conservative activities).
>
> Learns by taking initiative, exploring hidden possibilities, relying on intuition, self-discovery, constructing concepts, synthesizing content.
>
> Learners respond to spontaneity, free flow, experiential opportunities, experimentation, playfulness, future-orientated case discussions, visual displays, individuality.
>
> Organizers – the safe-keeping self.

3. Lower left quadrant B

> Likes order, planning, administration, organization, reliability, detail, low level of uncertainty (as opposed to holistic thinking, conceptualizing, synthesis, creating or innovating).
>
> Learns by organizing and structuring content, sequencing content, evaluating and testing theories, acquiring skills through practice, implementing course content.
>
> Learners respond to thorough planning, sequential order, organizational and administrative case discussions, textbooks, behaviour modification, programmed learning, structure and lectures.
>
> Humanitarians – the feeling self.

4. Lower right quadrant C

> Likes interpersonal, verbal, people-orientated, emotional, musical activities (as opposed to analytical technical, logical, mathematical activities).
>
> Learns by listening and sharing ideas, integrating experiences with self, moving and feeling, harmonizing with the content, emotional involvement.
>
> Learners respond to experiential opportunities, sensory movement, music, people-orientated case discussions, group interaction.

Right brain/left brain?

This questionnaire will give you an indication of your tendency to be a left brain learner, a right brain learner, or a bilateral learner (using both about equally). You could try this with your learners.

Directions: Answer the questions carefully, checking whether the answer is correct for you. Select the one that most closely represents your attitude or behaviour. When you have finished, refer to the scoring instructions.

---

1. I prefer to learn
   (a) details and specific facts
   (b) from a general overview of things and by looking at the whole picture
   (c) both ways about equally

⇨

2. I prefer the jobs

    (a) which consist of one task at a time, and I can complete it before beginning the next one
    (b) in which I work on many things at once
    (c) I like both kinds of jobs equally

3. I prefer to solve problems with

    (a) logic
    (b) my 'gut feelings'
    (c) both logic and 'gut feelings'

4. I like my work to be

    (a) planned so that I know exactly what to do
    (b) open with opportunities for change as I go along
    (c) both planned and open to change

5. I like to learn a movement in sports or dance better by

    (a) hearing a verbal explanation and repeating the action or step mentally
    (b) watching and then trying to do it
    (c) watching and then imitating and talking about it

6. I remember faces easily:

    (a) No
    (b) Yes
    (c) Sometimes

7. If I have to decide whether an issue is right or correct,

    (a) I decide on the basis of information
    (b) I instinctively feel it is right or correct
    (c) I tend to use a combination of both

8. I prefer

    (a) multiple-choice tests
    (b) essay tests
    (c) I like both kinds of tests equally

9. If I had to assemble a bicycle, I would most likely

    (a) lay out all the parts, count them, gather the necessary tools and follow directions
    (b) glance at the diagram and begin with whatever tools were there, sensing how the parts fit
    (c) recall past experiences in similar situations

10. At school, I preferred

    (a) algebra
    (b) geometry
    (c) I had no real preference of one over the other

11. It is more exciting to

    (a) improve something
    (b) invent something
    (c) Both are exciting to me

12. I generally

    (a) use time to organise work and personal activities
    (b) have difficulty in pacing personal activities to time limits
    (c) am able to pace personal activities to time limits with ease

⇨

13. Daydreaming is

    (a) a waste of time
    (b) a usable tool for planning my future
    (c) amusing and relaxing

14. I can tell fairly accurately how much time has passed without looking at a clock.

    (a) Yes
    (b) No
    (c) Sometimes

15. When reading or studying, I

    (a) prefer total quiet
    (b) prefer music
    (c) listen to background music only when reading for enjoyment, not while studying3p4

Scoring Instructions

Calculate the number of your 'A' and 'B' answers. Do not consider your 'C' answers.
Put a – (minus) sign in front of your 'A' score and a + (plus) sign in front of your 'B' score.
Do the algebraic sum of your 'A' and 'B' scores.

Scores

−15 to −13 = left brain dominant (very strong)
−12 to −9 = left brain dominant
−8 to −5 = moderate preference for the left
−4 to −1 = slight preference towards the left
0 = whole brain dominance (bilateral)
+1 to +4 = slight preference towards the right dominance (bilateral)
+5 to +8 = moderate preference for the right
+9 to +12 = right brain dominant
+13 to +15 = right brain dominant (very strong)

Sources: Questionnaire: Author unknown. Revisions by E. C. Davis (1994),
English Teaching Forum 32, 3, revised by Luciano Mariani (1996).

What do your scores on the left brain, right brain questionnaire mean?

'Left brain learners' (verbal sequential or serialist learner): You have a preference for learning in a sequential style, doing things logically step by step. You like to be organized and ordered in your approach and like to break things down into categories and to consider these separately. You are good at deductive thinking in terms of cause and effect. You like to do 'one thing at a time'. You like attending to detail. Those with a very strong left brain preference may lack imagination.

The following are serial strategies adopted by left brain learners (left brain approach):

step-by-step approach,
narrow focus,
deal with steps in order and in isolation,
like rules and structure,
logical rather than intuitive,
factual rather than using their own experience,
works from small steps up to the big picture.

'Right brain learners' (visual or holistic learner): You like to see things in the round and consider the whole. You focus on similarities, patterns and connections with former learning. You like to get a 'feel' for a topic and see how it all fits together. You prefer to follow your intuition rather than work things out carefully. You can use lateral thinking. You are flexible and like to use your imagination and be creative. Those with a very strong right brain preference may be disorganized.

Right brain students tend to adopt holistic strategy, which are listed below:

broad, global approach;
idiosyncratic, personalized and intuitive;
like to jump in anywhere;
impatient of rules, structure and details;
likes anecdotes, illustration and analogy.

Ideally, of course, students should be able to use both strategies and adopt whichever is most appropriate to the task at hand. Ross Cooper has shown that some students are not able to do this and that this inhibits their learning considerably. The difference between 'left' and 'right' brain thinking is summarised in Table 1.2.

Table 1.2 Summary of the left brain and right brain strengths

Left brain	Right brain
Verbal and sequential	Visual and holistic
Sees things in parts – sequential, language and logic	Sees things as a whole – spatial, music and images
Detail	Overview
Ordered	Speedy
Analytic	Imaginative
Critical	Creative
Logical	Lateral
Deductive	Inductive
Abstract	Symbolic
Elements	Patterns
Cause and effect	Interrelationships

Right brain teaching strategies: Cynthia Klein showed that teachers tend to use 'left brain' strategies, neglecting or devaluing many of the following right brain strategies. These help all students:

Overviews

Summaries, reviews, overviews, key points

Case studies, demonstrations, anecdotes, which show 'the whole' in context

Models, systems, for example, flow diagrams which describe the whole succinctly

'Advanced organizers', in other words, advanced summaries of what is about to be covered in a topic, especially if students are asked to recall prior learning and experience that might help with what they are about to learn

'Same and different' analysis: the learner determining what is the same and what is different when comparing two concepts, especially a known with one being learned

Visual thinking

Mindmaps, especially when used to summarize a topic

Other methods of structuring information, such as thinking frames, writing frames

Visual representations, posters, pictures, images, graphs, charts

Use of colour, shape and patterns

Fantasy

Metaphor, analogy, simile, symbol

Imagining 'What would it have been like to be a monk in an Abbey?'

Guided fantasy: 'Imagine you are a water molecule in a heated saucepan'

Acting/role play

Evocative language/feelings

Emotion, humour, appeal to senses

Personal feelings and associations

Direct experience

Doing things physically, hands on, manipulating, moving

Primary sources, real objects

Finding out for oneself

Excursions

Explorations and experiments

'Shadowing'

Role play and simulations

Multisensory learning

Feeling, touching, seeing, smelling

Hearing, sounds, rhythm and music

How can we accommodate for differences between our learners?

Completion of appropriate documentation during induction and early into the course may ensure that appropriate and regular support is given to learners. This documentation includes the devising of personal and individual learning plans that can be agreed with the learners and used to set targets. It is also important to plan lessons carefully in order to allow for particular needs. This may require you to organize specialist support for learners by liaising with other support networks inside and outside the organization.

Case Study

Nazia is 16 and came from Pakistan 5 years ago. She attended an English secondary School where she developed good speaking and listening skills. She speaks Urdu and Punjabi and is literate in Urdu. Her main difficulty is reading and writing English. She wants to develop her literacy skills but is worried about feeling culturally isolated at a large college of further education. She is very motivated and eventually wants to go into nursery teaching.

> What are some of the barriers which might prevent her from learning?
> How can some of these barriers be overcome?

Case Study

Ann works as a classroom assistant in a primary school. She originally went as a parent helper when her own children were young. When the staff discovered her abilities in art and craft, she was encouraged to apply for a post when one became available. Ann has been working in the school for 3 years and loves her job. Now, with the National Numeracy Strategy, classroom assistants are being given more responsibility working with children on literacy and numeracy.

Ann always found maths difficult at school. She was verbally abused by a maths teacher at one point in her school life and since then has had a 'mental block' about anything to do with numbers. The thought of attending the training course for classroom assistants on the numeracy strategy makes her feel physically sick, and she is thinking of resigning from her job although she loves the work. As a single parent, this would have a major impact on her financial circumstances. She becomes tearful when discussing her numeracy difficulties and does not know which way to turn.

> What are some of the barriers which might prevent her from learning?
> How can some of these barriers be overcome?

Feedback

Some of the main points from the case studies identify these common barriers: time, family commitments, special needs, learning difficulties, past experiences of education, culture, finance and accessibility.

Individual learning plans (ILPs)

Schools and colleges are now all using individual learning plans (paper and electronic) with young people aged 14 and over to support progression planning. The aims of the plans are as follows:

> review learning and progress;
> raise aspirations and motivation;
> inform choices;
> establish personal, learning and career goals.

Plans are developed in different ways, but all involve a supported process of individual planning and review. Students on Initial Teacher Training programmes also gain experience of ILPs by keeping their own ILPs throughout their programme. They may also work with their learners on reviewing, updating and action planning/target setting.

An example of ILP is shown below:

> ILP: Record of diagnostic assessment (ILT, numeracy, & literacy).
> Career plan: Where do you see yourself in 1 year's time? What skills/networking will you require in order achieve this goal?
> Personal skills: This section requires you to recognize existing skills you have acquired, including academic, language, literacy and numeracy, which you think may be of assistance to you in your teaching role.
> Strengths:
> Areas for development:

How are the above points important to you in your training/teaching role?

Initial assessment action plan

Key area	Present level	Action	By whom (this could include extra support)	Review date
Communication				
Application of number – numeracy				
ICT				
Literacy				
Study skills (include research, academic writing, Harvard referencing)				

Working with others				
Problem solving				
Improving own learning and performance				
Subject specialist knowledge				
Teaching ability (highlight where you think you are)	Grade 1 – outstanding Grade 2 – good Grade 3 – satisfactory Grade 4 – unsatisfactory			

Short-term/long-term goals				
Goals (identify short- and long-term goals; where do you see yourself in 1 year's time? keep these goals smart)	By (when? time given to each goal)	Activity (what do you need to do to get to your goal)	Resources (what will help you on your way? Tutor support, mentor support, group, external agencies etc?)	Done (review when goals have been achieved)

Tutor review of progress			
Area for development (from your initial assessments)	What progress have you made?	What do you need to do before the next review?	Tutors comments Signed: Date:

The importance of an ILP

An effective individual learning plan (ILP) is at the heart of assessment, learning, support and achievement. It helps the learner to become an active, motivated partner in learning. The ILP is

- a personalized, flexible route map to guide each learner's journey;
- a dynamic working document, owned and used by the learner, supported by teachers, employers and others;
- a record of learning goals and progression routes, initial and diagnostic assessment information, learning targets, progress and achievements within different contexts for learning;
- a communication aid between the learner and others who support the learning process in various contexts;
- a way of making and reinforcing links and connections between topics, subject and personal, learning and thinking skills.

In practice, this means learners are using their ILP to

> record what they want to achieve on their learning journey – their goals and progression options;
> negotiate and plan exactly what they are going to do, how and when.

The ILP will include

> learning targets with outcomes and time scales, and details of how success will be determined (success criteria);
> details of the resources, support and guidance the learner will use;
> details of where and how the learning will take place;
> view every assessment as a learning opportunity and to plan for the next steps in learning.

Reflection should be made on the following:

> What, and how, they learned.
> What went well and why.
> What went less well and why.
> Where they could use the skills and approaches again.

The benefits of ILPs

Learners can use ILPs to

> take ownership of their own learning;
> recognize the value of prior experiences;
> make sense of new experiences and understand how they learn;
> plan to practise skills and gain confidence by applying them in a range of different contexts, such as the workplace, at home or in the community;
> identify and understand barriers to learning and where they can find support to remove them;
> measure their own success.

Teachers can use ILPs to

> listen to learners' voices, review performance and respond to learners' needs;
> integrate processes around the learner: initial and diagnostic assessment, action planning, learner contracts, additional support needs, tutorial records, learner performance, progression options and exit information;
> match teaching and learning to learners' strengths and needs, and ensure that learners are on the right programmes and achieving according to expectations;
> plan opportunities for learners to extend their learning into contexts such as the workplace, community or leisure activities;
> plan opportunities for progression to further learning.

The Lifelong Learning Sector and educare

Anthony Giddens (2004) argues that the concept of 'partnership' characterizes New Labour's approach to social policy. This means that all the sectors of the 'mixed economy of care' (statutory, private, voluntary and informal) are now encouraged to work together. Tony Blair was voted into power in 1997, and a consequence has been the emphasis that is placed on 'educare'. This means that those working within education, health and social care are encouraged to work in cooperation. A number of issues have impacted upon the Lifelong Learning Sector. Teachers are expected to adopt teaching and learning strategies that are supportive of 'partnership' and 'working together as part of a team'.

The main emphasis in general is placed on the sectors that provide services for the community working together. These sectors are traditionally referred to as the statutory, private, voluntary and informal sectors.

Activity 1.2

Write out a definition for the statutory, private, voluntary and informal sectors.

Feedback

Table1.3 defines the statutory, private, voluntary and informal sectors.

Table 1.3 Defining the mixed economy of care

Sector of care	Definition	Examples
Statutory	The statutory sector includes all of the services that are financed and organized by the government.	Examples of statutory services include schools, the National Health Service (NHS), and state social services.
Private	The private sector includes all of the services that operate to make a financial profit.	Examples of private services include private nurseries and private schools.
Voluntary	The voluntary sector operates according to 'good will'.	Voluntary organizations include charities such as 'Barnados' and 'Childline'.
Informal	The informal sector is characterized by family and friends caring for each other because of 'love' and/or 'obligation'.	Parents caring for children and friends caring for each other are examples of 'informal' care.

This model of care has evolved due to a number of social, political, historical and economic factors. It has resulted in educational initiatives that encourage 'cooperation' and 'consensus' becoming popular. Two example initiatives that impact on the Lifelong Learning Sector are *mentoring* and *multiple intelligences*.

Mentoring

Alcock, Payne, and Sullivan (2000: 321) argue that a main feature of New Labour's approach to educational policy is to 'reinforce a greater role for parents'. This indicates that the traditional model of educational power has changed. As opposed to emphasizing the autonomy of educational professionals, the focus is placed on a more equalitarian approach to education in which educators work alongside other professionals and communities to enable what Alcock, Payne, and Sullivan (2000: 321) refer to as 'joined up solutions to joined up problems'. This has meant that 'mentoring' has become an important component of the professional work of the Lifelong Learning Sector.

In this context, mentoring can be understood as meaning 'the support given by one, (usually more experienced) person for the growth and learning of another' (Malderez, 2001: 57). From 2005 onwards, OFSTED have emphasized the importance of mentoring so that novices are 'nurtured' by more experienced 'experts'. This point is discussed by Ingleby and Hunt (2008) in their analysis of mentoring within the Lifelong Learning Sector.

Strengths and weaknesses of mentoring

It can be argued that the 'joined-up solutions' approach to 'joined-up problems' within the Lifelong Learning Sector is worthwhile. This point is supported by Brookes (2005: 43) who argues that the importance of mentoring was identified by Bell and Lancaster in 1805. In other words, an effective mentoring system has been identified as being an important component of education for many years. It can be argued that effective education in the Lifelong Learning Sector is likely to benefit from applying 'the lessons of experience'. This means that there is nothing wrong with the principle of emphasizing the importance of mentoring. What becomes more questionable is whether mentoring is being recommended as an integral part of education; yet there is no clear understanding of the model of mentoring that needs to be introduced. This is again reported in the research of Ingleby and Hunt (2008). It appears to suggest that although mentoring is emphasized as being an important component of collaboration and partnership, the mechanisms for introducing and applying mentoring into the Lifelong Learning Sector are unclear and ambiguous.

Activity 1.3

Give an appraisal of New Labour's 'mentoring' policy.

Feedback

It can be argued that policy becomes ineffective if it is nothing more than 'window dressing'. In other words, if all the policy does is to 'look good on the outside', it will never meet complex needs. This may appear to be the case with 'mentoring'. It is a policy approach that 'makes sense on the outside'.

⇨

It appears to be a 'good idea' until one asks questions about how mentoring is to be effectively implemented. The Ingleby and Hunt (2008) research raises five issues about the effectiveness of mentoring. These points are as follows: The role of the mentor needs clarification; mentors need to be more aware of the educational aims of academic programmes; uncertainty is present over mentor training needs; mentor training is inconsistent; professional boundaries between mentors and mentees are underdeveloped. This appears to suggest that the policy of mentoring can only become a part of 'collaboration' and 'partnership' if these questions are answered.

Multiple intelligences

Alcock, Payne, and Sullivan (2000: 321) argue that New Labour's partnership approach to society emphasizes the importance of 'values of community, responsibility and social solidarity'. A consequence of this approach for the Lifelong Learning Sector is to view educators and those being educated as 'working together'. This has had consequences for those who would have previously been unable to adjust to the demands of the educational system, for example, learners with 'challenging behaviour' and 'special educational needs'. The consequence of the partnership model is that, as opposed to excluding learners who cannot meet the demands of the education system, another approach is needed. This requires the education system to adapt to the needs of learners who have previously been excluded.

A consequence of this approach is the implementation of learning strategies that are based on the ideas of Howard Gardner (1984, 1993, 2000). Gardner proposes that there are eight forms of intelligence. These are 'visual spatial', 'linguistic', 'logical mathematical', 'musical', 'bodily kinaesthetic', 'interpersonal', 'intrapersonal' and 'naturalistic' intelligence. Supporters of Gardner's ideas (e.g., OFSTED) argue that the traditional educational system is based on 'linguistic' and 'logical mathematical' intelligence. The argument runs that the Lifelong Learning Sector can be more inclusive if it acknowledges other categories of intelligence and in turn incorporates activities to develop these 'other' skills and abilities. This has led to the introduction of 'learning inventories' that attempt to identify the preferred learning style of groups of learners.

Strengths and weaknesses of 'multiple intelligences'

The attention that has been given to multiple intelligences can be seen as being positive if it leads to a more innovative curriculum for the Lifelong Learning Sector. Frank Coffield's (2004) research into learning styles does acknowledge that there are potential benefits in establishing learning inventories. This allows the possibility of tailoring teaching and learning in order to meet the needs of the learners. As opposed to making the curriculum an aspect of education that is 'followed by the learners', increased awareness of learning styles can allow for more innovative teaching and learning activities. If the group's learning preference is predominantly 'visual spatial', this can be used to justify 'visual spatial' learning activities. Coffield's (2004) research also gives a critique of learning styles. It is possible to ask, 'Why are there eight types of intelligence?' Why not nine or ten or more? Another critique of the implementation of learning inventories is that it adds on another layer of bureaucracy to the heavily bureaucratic teaching profession. This may mean that being aware of learning styles becomes more of an aspect of 'audit' to impress OFSTED inspectors than an innovative part of the Lifelong Learning Sector.

Activity 1.4

Give an appraisal of New Labour's acceptance of 'multiple intelligences'.

Feedback

Coffield's (2004) research appears to question the validity of the concept of 'multiple intelligences'. This argument can be developed to question the nature of the Lifelong Learning Sector's policy-making process. Critics of educational policy making, such as Lucas (2007), argue that too much education is 'standards driven'. This means that the educational process is not being fully acknowledged. The literal meaning of the word 'education' implies that the individual is enabled to see the world differently. This is less likely to happen if education becomes 'standards driven'. If multiple intelligences are applied to education to impress OFSTED, this will not mean that they become an integral part of learning. They are instead akin to bureaucratic tasks that are standards driven as opposed to being designed to educate individuals in the truest sense of the term. Coffield (2004) argues for a return to the notion of 'Platonic kings', in other words, for educationalists who are experts in practice and in turn able to shape educational policies. Perhaps this idea should be at the centre of future Lifelong Learning Sector policies.

Activity 1.5

When you are next on the internet, do a word search for 'mentoring' and 'multiple intelligences'. Try to find out more information about these two aspects of New Labour policy. Make a note of how the areas of policy affect your own Lifelong Learning setting by considering the following two case studies.

Case Study

Catherine has had an eating disorder (anorexia nervosa) since she was 16. She is now 42 and she has never been able to have a permanent relationship. Although she wants to have children, she is not able to have a family due to her debilitating eating disorder. Catherine is consciously aware of her eating disorder, but she cannot explain why she has this condition. She does not know anyone else in her family who has an eating disorder. Catherine has tried a number of different forms of counselling including Rogerian therapy, but the counselling has been unable to help. This led to Catherine paying for psychodynamic counselling. The counselling sessions appeared to help her because they focused on the link existing between Catherine's conscious and unconscious mind. The counsellor explained to Catherine that she was experiencing an oral fixation and that her conscious eating disorder could be traced back to her unconscious mind. Catherine was adopted at birth. It was proposed that Catherine's eating disorder was a consequence of being adopted at birth. Catherine found the counselling most helpful. The counselling sessions led her to contact her natural mother. The subsequent meetings meant that Catherine's conscious thoughts were more positive. This helped in promoting a more positive self-perception. Although the therapy worked, Catherine sometimes wondered if her conscious eating disorder could really be traced to a time in her life she could not remember. It seemed a bizarre explanation for her conscious thoughts. At present, Catherine is studying a 'Basic Skills' programme at her local college.

Feedback

There are many learners in the Lifelong Learning Sector who can have complex learning needs. Learners who display 'challenging behaviour' may exhibit behaviour like this because of the difficulties they are experiencing. Learners like 'Catherine' may not be 'typical students', but you may have to work with learners who have all sorts of complex emotional needs. If this is the case, it is very helpful to have a 'mentor', in other words, someone who can give you advice and support. Ideally, your mentor will be assigned to you formally so that you have a colleague at your side who can give you help and assistance. If mentoring is used for this purpose, then it can be claimed that it is an excellent part of the Lifelong Learning Sector. If, however, the mentoring relationship is part of the audit process to please the inspectorate, it may mean that effective support mechanisms are not in place to help staff who are working with complex learners.

Case Study

Michael is 16 and he has a number of forms of challenging behaviour that mean that he can be physically aggressive. Michael's tutor (Steven) finds this behaviour very difficult, so the communication strategies that are applied to the relationship are especially important. Steven believes in a number of values that may be described as 'old fashioned'. He thinks that aggressive behaviour is 'bad behaviour'. This means that Steven's verbal and nonverbal communication with Michael can be negative. The other staff who work with Michael are aware of the tension that appears to exist between Steven and Michael. One staff member, Susan, suggested that Steven's way of communicating with Michael actually made Michael's challenging behaviour worse. It led Susan to conclude that Michael's needs would only be met if he had staff working with him who could meet his many complex learning needs.

⇨

Feedback

If Michael's learning preferences are identified, this may help him to become an effective learner in the Lifelong Learning Sector. At present, Michael has never done well in formal education. His tutors may be able to help him if they can identify how Michael learns. Perhaps Michael is a 'visual' learner, and if the learning materials are presented to him in this way this may help his future learning? It can also be argued that this process of identifying individual learning preferences is very time consuming. The Lifelong Learning Sector is not characterized by limitless resources that allow for every individual's learning needs to be assessed and readily met. This can mean that 'multiple intelligences' becomes more of an ideal as opposed to being a 'reality'!

Summary of key points

In this chapter, we have looked at the key areas of the Preparing to Teach in the Lifelong Learning Sector Award. The chapter began by identifying the key characteristics of a good teacher and focusing on the quality of teaching and learning. The section on planning learning identified a simple session plan design with detailed information on how to plan and evaluate sessions. This was followed by an overview of barriers to learning that some students face and how we can use initial assessment information to create an Individual Learning Plan. The chapter ended by explaining the relationship between the Lifelong Learning Sector and 'educare'. The emphasis that is now placed upon cooperation and multi-agency working may mean that it is important for you to be aware that you are part of a wider team that is trying to meet the needs of a diverse range of learners.

This chapter links to the following SVUK professional standards:

Professional values

AS 4: Reflection and evaluation of their own practice and their continuing professional development as teachers
AS 7: Improving the quality of their practice
BS 1: Maintaining an inclusive, equitable and motivating learning environment

Professional knowledge and understanding

AK 1.1: What motivates learners to learn and the importance of learners' experience and aspirations
AK 3.1: Issues of equality, diversity and inclusion
AK 4.1: Principles, frameworks and theories which underpin good practice in learning and teaching
AK 4.2: The impact of own practice on individuals and their learning
BK 1.1: Ways to maintain a learning environment in which learners feel safe and supported

⇨

Professional practice

AP 4.2: Reflect on and demonstrate commitment to improvement of own personal and teaching skills through regular evaluation and use of feedback

AP 4.3: Share good practice with others and engage in continuing professional development through reflection, evaluation and appropriate use of research

AP 7.3: Use feedback to develop own practice within the organization's systems

BP 1.1: Establish a purposeful learning environment where learners feel safe, secure, confident and valued

---

Self-assessment questions

Question 1: What are the skills and qualities of a good teacher?
Question 2: What are the key features of a good lesson plan?
Question 3: Give an example of how to evaluate a teaching session?

Moving on feature

This chapter has introduced the practicalities of planning and evaluating lessons. The next chapter on teaching in the sector will enable you to apply some of this theory into reflecting further and becoming a professional within the sector.

Further Reading

Fawbert, F. (2003), *Teaching in Post-Compulsory Education: Learning, Skills and Standards*. London: Continuum.

Petty, G. (1998), *Teaching Today (2nd Edition)*. Cheltenham: Nelson Thornes.

Wallace, S. (2007), *Teaching Tutoring and Training in the Lifelong Learning Sector*. Exeter, UK: Learning Matters.

An excellent textbook that is written in an accessible way and makes clear links to applying theory to practice.

References

Alcock, C., Payne, S. & Sullivan, M. (2000), *Introducing Social Policy*. Harlow: Prentice Hall.

Brookes, W. (2005), 'The graduate teacher programme in England: mentor training, quality assurance and the findings of inspection'. *Journal of In-Service Education*, 31, 43–61.

Coffield, F. (2004), *Should We Be Using Learning Styles?* London: Learning and Skills Research Centre.

Gardner, H. (1984), *Frames of Mind: The Theory of Multiple Intelligence*. New York: Basic Books.

Gardner, H. (1993), *Multiple Intelligences: The Theory in Practice*. New York: Basic Books Limited.

Gardner, H. (2000), *Intelligence Reframed: Multiple Intelligences for the 21st Century*. New York: Basic Books.

Giddens, A. (2004), *The third way and its critics*. Cambridge: Polity Press.

Ingleby, E. and Hunt, J. (2008), 'The CPD needs of mentors in initial teacher training in England'. *Journal of In-Service Education*, 34, 61–74.

Lucas, N. (2007), 'The in-service training of adult literacy, numeracy, and English for speakers of other languages: the challenges of a 'standards led model'. *Journal of In-Service Education*, 33, 125–142.

Malderez, A. (2001), 'New ELT professionals'. *English Teaching Professional*, 19, 57–58.

Petty, G. (1998), *Teaching Today (2nd Edition)*. Cheltenham: Nelson Thornes.

Reece, I. and Walker, S. (2007), *Teaching Training and Learning: A Practical Guide*. Sunderland, UK: Business Education Publishers.

Teaching in the Learning and Skills Sector

Chapter Outline

Learning Outcomes

After reading this chapter you should be able to

identify the differences between different teaching and learning strategies,
analyse the differences between teacher- and student-centred learning,
identify different forms of assessment,
develop reflective practice and make links to continuous professional development.

Introduction

This chapter reflects on teaching and learning in a variety of educational contexts. The chapter provides an introduction to continuous professional development. The chapter also discusses in detail different forms of assessment and the value of using a range of strategies.

Alongside exploring key themes such as 'reflective practice', the chapter acknowledges that a variety of learners are present within the Lifelong Learning Sector. This necessitates knowledge of a range of teaching and learning strategies. The chapter also links to 'classroom management', and this topic is discussed later in the book.

Teaching and learning strategies

During the first chapter, we discussed the importance of identifying students' learning styles. One method we used for this was Herrmann's whole brain model (1982). This method can help us to identify left brain, right brain and whole brain thinkers. This information can be applied to identifying teaching strategies which would suit whole brain and right brain thinkers and develop the more creative and imaginative aspects of left brain learners. In order to review Herrmann's model in relation to choosing appropriate teaching and learning strategies, an overview of the differences between left and right brain thinkers follows.

Left brain thinkers are categorized as being theorists and organizers. The theorists enjoy logical, rational concepts. They like acquiring facts, analysing and forming theories. The organizers enjoy order, so they need clear planning and structure but also linkage to the practical application of facts.

Right brain thinkers are the innovators and humanitarians. The innovators are creative and imaginative; they enjoy self-discovery and exploring concepts and experimenting with new ideas. The humanitarians enjoy working with people as they have good listening skills and share ideas with others; they also can make emotional involvements.

Once students' learning styles have been identified, it is a teacher's responsibility to develop learners' weaker preferences to develop a whole brain approach. For example, if you have a number of left brain theorists in your group, you would need to carefully integrate right brain activities with clear and logical instructions and outcomes to make the learning experience as thorough as possible.

Range of teaching and learning strategies

The range of teaching methods from which teachers can choose is vast. Here are some examples:

Lecture: It is useful with large groups of learners, where participation is limited because of time or number of learners. This requires minimal participation or interaction with learners and didactic or tutor-centred delivery. Teaching is used to transfer large amounts of information in a limited time frame to a maximum number of students. This teaching strategy is predominantly used in Higher Education teaching.

Presentation: This is similar to the lecture in that the strategy is to transfer large amounts of information; however, the groups tend to be smaller. The maximum time spent on a presentation without any group interaction should be kept to 20 minutes. PowerPoint slides now often accompany the tutor presentation. Try to ensure that you are not tempted to overload slides with information or read line for line from the PowerPoint. The presentation is a tutor-centred strategy, but it should be used alongside discussion/Q&A techniques. Effective presentations rely on the tutor having a charismatic style in order to make the presentations memorable.

Demonstration: It is used to show practical skills. They need to be logically delivered with clear instructions. Longer practical activities need to be broken in to segments to ensure whole group understanding. Ensure learner errors are checked and addressed early to ensure that 'bad habits' do not become a form of learnt behaviour! These demonstrations are often used in vocational and practical teaching programmes. They can be 'tutor centred' in the demonstration section of the session.

Discussion: Ideas, opinions, beliefs and knowledge are shared freely within whole group or small group in discussions. They are useful when meeting affective domain learning outcomes as the tutor can assess achievement of changing or confirming values, opinions, beliefs. Tutors need to keep learners focused on the topic or can guide learners discussions into deeper learning for enrichment. Discussion is a useful strategy to use to consolidate small/whole group activities or during introductions/conclusions to sessions. Discussions are often a student-centred teaching and learning strategy.

Question and answer: This strategy is similar to 'discussions', but an advantage is that you can pose questions to the whole group and also to individuals. Posing questions to individuals (once you know your learners) helps to differentiate learning. You can pose questions to individuals that you know as they can answer the questions to boost confidence and to develop whole group speaking skills. You can use higher order questions to offer challenge and to develop evaluation, analysis and application skills. Q&A is useful for introducing and concluding sessions; also during the use of another strategy, for example, during demonstrations, questions can be asked to maintain focus and interest and assess the learners' understanding of the task.

Brainstorming: Learners are given a topic or question with thinking time allocated. Responses are then called out to a 'scribe' who notes comments on flip chart, wipe board or interactive wipe boards. (Interactive boards are a very useful resource for this strategy as the feedback can be saved and printed for the group or uploaded to an organization's Virtual Learning Environment [VLE]). Good classroom management skills are needed to maintain focus on the given topic. This is another example of a student-centred teaching and learning strategy.

Seminar: These are often used in Higher Education following a lecture where the content of the lecture can be dissected and discussed with activities that apply the learning to a particular situation. Seminars can be an opportunity for small groups to work together investigating a topic and presenting back to the whole group. Good classroom management skills are needed to ensure all learners, within the small groups, are working on topic set and that it is not led by one or two group members. This is also a student-centred learning and teaching strategy.

Tutorials: Small group or individual tutorials are a useful strategy to determine the progress of learners on the programme. Tutorials are often used to review individual learning plans by identifying achievements of previous action plans. They can give an opportunity to set new individualized targets. Sufficient time may not be available to cover both personal and course-based issues. Learners also need to be encouraged to plan for their tutorials by ensuring that they have thought about their ILP development and what targets or issues they have outstanding. This teaching and learning strategy can be tutor centred; however, more involvement with the learner to set their own personalized targets is likely to ensure that the strategy becomes more learner centred.

Practical: This could take the form of student practice work following a demonstration. Learners use the instruction given to develop subject skills. These are often assessed against summative performance criteria set by an awarding body, or they may be formatively assessed against specific learning outcomes. Tutors facilitate the practical work observing and correcting skills as necessary. Once again, this is a student-centred teaching and learning strategy.

Simulation and games: Simulation is where learners undertake a task involving the same procedures as would be needed in a real-life situation. The simulation needs to be realistic and can often be expensive to resource. Simulations are often used in practical subjects such as 'First Aid'.

Games can take many forms, for example, from 'card sorting' and 'word searches' to more interactive games using the interactive white board. Games such as 'Who Wants to Be a Millionaire' and 'Blockbusters' may be adapted as teaching and learning activities. Good planning and resourcing skills are needed to ensure that the games are interesting, motivating and add enjoyment to focused learning. This is usually a student-centred approach to teaching and learning.

Role play: In this strategy, learners practice being in a specific role and act out a particular situation which is close to real life. Role play is often used for 'customer services' and 'counselling' training. Learners need to have sufficient background information to act out situations and roles, or the experience may leave them lacking confidence and/or embarrassed. Another area to consider is that some learners may not take the role play seriously. This is a student-centred teaching and learning strategy.

Films and TV programmes: Using film/TV clips (whether from DVDs or the Internet) can add a break to the norm in teaching sessions. Selecting the right amount of 'clip' is crucial to ensure the meaning is maintained without becoming tiresome. 'Youtube' and 'TeachersTV' have become a useful resource bank for teachers to use in the classrooms. 'TeachersTV' in particular have clips which are separated into curriculum areas. Again good classroom management skills are needed to ensure there is a purpose to the learners watching the clips, with the facilitation of a subsequent discussion about the content. This teaching and learning strategy is more tutor centred.

Distance learning: This is where learners are studying away from the main campus; this could be within the United Kingdom or abroad. Distance learning can be particularly useful where access to conventional courses is restricted, for example, for geographic or for domestic or work reasons. Many universities are offering their programmes to international institutions with the programme leaders based in the United Kingdom. Learners can work through material set with tutorial support via e-mail, block attendance weeks or telephone. Where learners are well motivated, this may work well. Resources need to be high quality and electronically available to support individual students' needs. This is another student-centred approach to learning and teaching.

Discovery projects/research: Learners are set tasks (that would generally take a longer time span) via self-directed learning. They may be individual or small group tasks with the tutor taking on a tutorial/facilitation role guiding and advising students to keep the learners focused. 'Target setting' is important to ensure deadlines are met with successful achievement of tasks. Learners gain a wider range of skills, including working with others, taking responsibility for own learning, problem solving and communication skills development. An active style of learning may encourage poorly motivated learners. Careful monitoring may be needed as some learners may do very little to contribute to the task. This is a student-centred approach to learning and teaching.

When a teacher/trainer makes decisions about the methods or strategies to employ, the effectiveness of the choice involves the following:

suitability of methods for promoting the intended learning;
variety, both within learning sessions and in a programme;
economy of effort relative to the leaning benefit;
human factors;
proper planning and resourcing within time constraints;
proper control and management of the learning process;
sufficient skill in using methodology (both teacher and students);
proper use of feedback, monitoring and flexibility;
assessment of learning, and evaluating process and outcomes.

One of the key factors that we need to consider when choosing teaching and learning methods is the preference of our learners and just how much they learn via a particular teaching strategy.

Table 2.1 indicates that, in general, students appear to enjoy active forms of learning. The table reveals that group discussions are 'highly liked' by learners and lectures are preferred the least. This is an area we must consider strongly when choosing teaching and

Table 2.1 Students' preferences in teaching styles

Style	Like (%)	Dislike (%)	Neutral (%)
Group discussion	80	4	17
Games/simulations	80	2	17
Drama	70	9	22
Artwork	67	9	26
Design	63	4	33
Experiments	61	11	28
Computers	59	22	20
Exploring feelings	59	11	30
Reading English literature	57	9	35
Practical ideas	52	9	37
Laboratory work	50	11	37
Library research	50	24	26
Charts, tables etc.	46	15	37
Craft work	43	17	39
Fieldwork	43	20	35
Open-ended work	43	20	37
Themes	41	11	48
Creating products	41	11	43
Working alone	41	26	33
Invention	39	20	41
Organizing data	37	20	43
Empathy	35	30	35
Observation	30	13	57
Worksheets	28	17	52
Reading for information	26	30	43
Using technology	24	26	46
Deadlines	24	50	26
Time schedules	17	41	41
Analysis	17	35	46
Theories	15	39	43
Essays	13	28	54
Lectures	11	70	19

Note: Data collected from questionnaires submitted by 11-18-year-old students, provided by M. Hebditch, Gillingham School Dorset, 1990.

learning strategies. The more active styles of learning are linked to right brain strategies, while the least student centred being left brain.

All learning may be regarded as being 'experiential'. Competence in the use of any methodology involves being able to choose intelligently, with the knowledge, experience and skill to make chosen methods work effectively.

If we consider just the learning styles/preferences of our learners, we can see that different methods are more suitable for different learning styles (Table 2.2). You have been learning about right brain and left brain thinking.

Table 2.2 Teaching methods

Activity 2.1

Create a list of teaching methods that will suit learners with right brain and left brain preferences.

Feedback

Teaching methods/strategies

Right brain	Left brain
Discussion	Lecture
Question and answer	Presentation
Brainstorming	Demonstration
Seminar	Tutorials
Tutorials	Film/TV clips
Practical	
Simulation	
Games	
Role play	
Distance learning	
Discovery learning/projects	
(You can add more to this list!)	

Tutor- or student-centred learning

Traditionally, teachers were at the centre of learning with students assuming a receptive role in their education. With research by authors such as Geoff Petty (1998) showing how people learn, traditional curriculum approaches to instruction where teachers were at the centre gave way to new ways of teaching and learning. A key theme among these changes is the idea that students actively construct their own learning (known as constructivism). The theorists John Dewey, Jean Piaget and Lev Vygotsky, whose collective work focuses on how students learn, are primarily responsible for this move to student-centred learning. Carl Rogers' (1969) ideas about the formation of the individual also contributed to student-centred learning. Student-centred learning means reversing the traditional teacher-centred understanding of the learning process and putting students at the centre of the learning process.

Teacher-centred learning

Traditionally, teachers have been seen as the 'fountains of all knowledge'. They may be regarded as allowing students to take a passive role in the session by delivering from the front of classroom. Sessions may be tutor led using lecture or presentation styles of delivery. Tutors traditionally dictated reams of notes, using overhead projected transparencies to assist the delivery, that they expected students to copy down. This can still be seen but perhaps using more 'up-to-date' resources through the use of PowerPoint, commonly known as 'death by PowerPoint'. Teacher-centred learning also follows strict rigid time frames, such as set times and dates, for the teaching delivery. These dates may be influenced by the 'awarding body' who have created the academic syllabus. The tutors may use a very didactic approach with the learning restricted to classroom-based delivery.

Student-centred learning

With student-centred learning, tutors take a 'back seat' and facilitate the learning experiences. Students adopt an active role in their learning by taking responsibility for their own achievements. Sessions are student led with flexible study patterns and a negotiated curriculum. Group learning, utilizing action plans closely monitored and facilitated by the tutor, attempts to ensure progress and achievement. Learning is not restricted to classroom, as there is the utilization of a range of teaching and learning strategies.

Benefits of student-centred learning

- For the learners:

  can work alone or in small groups, on and off campus;
  have access to a range of learning resources other than the tutor;
  can take exams at own convenience;
  can enrol at flexible times of the year;
  take ownership of their learning, become reflective learners and be empowered;
  are more motivated and committed towards learning because they become partners in the learning process;
  can work and learn in partnership.

- For the tutor:

  act as facilitators, guides, mentors;
  are able to work in teams and draw on the help from technicians, librarians;
  are able to work with students to determine teaching and learning strategies;
  develop student's ability to become a 'researcher', accessing multiple sources of information.

- For the organization:

  able to attract non-traditional students and students from diverse backgrounds;
  widen higher education (HE) participation into the community;
  more 'learners on seats (!)';
  opportunity to improve 'bottom-line' performance;
  gain international reputation;
  tutor time can be freed up to spend on research and attracting research funding

(*Source*: McLean [1997] and Educational Initiative Centre [2004]).

Limitations of student-centred learning

Work for students needs to be well planned and managed. Tasks need to be clear with the learning outcomes clearly stated. Management of activities needs careful monitoring and facilitating. Small group or individual tutorials are useful to check progress and set targets. It is important to allow learners to become involved with target setting as this again ensures learners are managing their progress alongside their own learning and development. Learners should be aware of the time scale for the tasks to ensure they take responsibility for time management and organization. The tasks should be resourced effectively so that if learners are working using learning resource centres or the internet for research, these resources need to be available and current in order to accommodate the project. Some student-centred learning approaches may not be suitable for all learners, for example, those with learning difficulties.

It can be argued that overall student-centred learning is driving institutions to develop 21st century approaches to learning. It can be an effective strategy to increase widening participation and facilitate lifelong learning initiatives. There are undoubtedly tangible benefits for students, tutors and institutions.

Assessment

Assessment is an integral part of the learning experience. Teachers, and learners themselves, are continually making judgements about their progress. Learners may be comparing their own achievements with those of others in ways which may or may not be helpful. Whether assessment is formal or informal, a dialogue about the criteria upon which assessments are made is needed. Assessment is probably one of the most important things we do as teachers; it enables learners to gain their qualifications.

Assessment is an ongoing process aimed at understanding and improving student learning. It involves making our expectations explicit and clear to our learners. This can mean setting appropriate criteria and high standards for learning quality. It can also mean systematically gathering, analysing and interpreting evidence to determine how well performance matches those expectations and standards. This in turn allows us to use the resulting information to document, explain and improve performance.

Why do we assess our learners?

We assess students for a number of reasons. We assess formatively to ensure learners have met the learning outcomes set for a particular session to perhaps reinforce the learning. We test students understanding and skills development through observation of practical exercises. During observations of practical tasks, we use set performance criteria to determine the level of student ability. Vocational programmes have set performance criteria devised by the awarding body. These can be national standards which all centres use to judge standards of performance.

During assessment activities, learners have the opportunity to apply the learning they have experienced within sessions to actual situations, whether it is through case studies, assignments, essays or practical assessments. Assessment can be both motivating and demotivating to learners. Petty (1998) in his model 'the learning engine' identifies how assessment can motivate by having success reinforced by tutor praise and feedback. This can in turn lead to self-praise, peer approval and 'self-belief' or an 'I can do it' feeling which raises self-confidence and self-esteem. This can motivate the learner and increase persistence and effort; hence work improves. The notion of 'success breeding success' is central to this idea. By contrast, if 'assessment failure' is experienced by the learner, this can lead to criticism. Both self-criticism and perhaps peer criticism with no tutor support may lead to falling self-belief. The student starts to believe 'I can't do it' with self-confidence and self-esteem being diminished. Motivation falls as does persistence and effort. The consequence can be a deterioration in standards of work. This may eventually lead to 'course failure' or 'withdrawal'.

Assessing students leads naturally into their expectation of gaining feedback. It can be argued that learning is an active process. To learn, we need to plan what we're going to do, attempt to do it and then receive feedback on our work. We then use this feedback to improve the work we have just done or, more often in education, to ensure that the next work we do embraces what we have learned. Feedback also affects how we feel about our work and inevitably also about ourselves. Feedback thus, as we have just previously identified, affects student motivation. Feedback remains essential. Students may even lose focus through the odd few minutes of a lecture or seminar, but they will read, pore over, analyse, debate, argue with and quite possibly treasure your feedback. This is especially true if the written feedback is useful! Giving good feedback is a skill which can be learned and honed. Some useful tips include the following:

> be clear and direct, whereby the reasons for assessment decisions are fully explained in language which is direct and unambiguous rather than vague or beating around the bush;
>
> constructive, because it is important to offer advice for further action which considers the student's academic capacity;
>
> descriptive of what the tutor has seen/observed/thinks rather than being over-evaluative or judgemental;
>
> helpful and supportive on the tutor's part (this attitude must be fully communicated to the student);
>
> well timed, being given as soon as possible after evidence has been demonstrated and at a time when the student is receptive to feedback;
>
> fully understood by the student, with the tutor making every effort to ensure this, leaving no unresolved questions, misunderstandings or conclusions;
>
> specific, being related to particular incidents or learning events (Armitage et al., 1999).

Good feedback has three key elements (Petty, 1998):

> A medal – describe positive aspects of the work (product or process).
> A mission – information about what needs improving and how to improve it. This needs to be forward looking and positive.
> Clear goal – set the students' tasks with assessment criteria.

How can you ensure every student earns a medal? Set attainable goals which are closely monitored and action planned. If you set a task and leave learners to do the task and they do not achieve as well as expected, could you have offered further tutorial support during the assessment process? It is important to ensure that tasks are broken down so that clear guidance is given to each section. Assessment guidance sheets are a good way of ensuring all learners are clear as to the expected elements needed for completion. It is helpful for some learners to see example answers to questions such as what is a distinction-level answer, a merit level and a pass level.

Recognizing partial success is also important to motivate and encourage self-esteem (remember the learning engine!) Recognize and give praise for the process the learners have gone through as well as the product they have produced. Some learners who are new or recently returning to education may have had to face some significant barriers to learning working towards the assessed piece. Never restrict praise or recognition to those with motivation, aptitude or flair!

Remember the final outcome of assessment is to allow students to progress and qualify.

Definitions of Key Terminology Used in Assessment

Assessment is often divided into formative and summative categories for the purpose of considering different objectives for assessment practices:

> Summative assessment is generally carried out at the end of a course or project. In an educational setting, summative assessments are typically used to assign students a course grade or completion of an award.
>
> Formative assessment is generally carried out throughout a lesson, course or project. Formative assessment, also referred to as 'educative assessment', is used to aid learning. In an educational setting, formative assessment might be done by a teacher (or peer) or the learner, providing feedback on a student's work, and would not necessarily be used for grading purposes.

Summative and formative assessments are often referred to in a learning context as *assessment of learning* and *assessment for learning,* respectively. Assessment of learning is generally summative in nature and intended to measure learning outcomes. This is in order to report those outcomes to students, parents and programme administrators. Assessment of learning generally occurs at the conclusion of a class, course, semester or academic year. Assessment for learning is generally formative in nature and is used by teachers to consider approaches to teaching and next steps for individual learners and the class.

⇨

> A common form of formative assessment is *diagnostic assessment*. Diagnostic assessment measures a student's current knowledge and skills for the purpose of identifying a suitable programme of learning. *Self-assessment* is a form of diagnostic assessment which involves students assessing themselves. *Forward-looking assessment* asks those being assessed to consider themselves in hypothetical future situations.

Objective and subjective

Assessment (either summative or formative) is often categorized as either objective or subjective. Objective assessment is a form of questioning which has a single correct answer. Subjective assessment is a form of questioning which may have more than one correct answer (or more than one way of expressing the correct answer). There are various types of objective and subjective questions. Objective-question types include true/false answers, multiple-choice, multiple-response and matching questions. Subjective questions include extended-response questions and essays. Objective assessment is well suited to the increasingly popular computerized or online assessment. A dictionary definition of an objective assessment is dealing with outward things or exhibiting facts uncoloured by feelings or opinions (Oxford Dictionary, 2009).

How can we make assessments objective?

Use a mark scheme: With any assessment method you should have a marking scheme which details the elements contained within the assessment. All markers should use the same scheme for consistency and reliability. It is good practice to ensure all students are aware of the marking scheme (this could be contained within the assessment brief) to give clear guidance as to what needs to be covered for a successful outcome. Once the assessments have been marked, moderators also use the same marking scheme/criteria to check whether all assessors are standardized in their approach to marking.

Use a check sheet or list: This is similar to the marking scheme but perhaps more simply shown as a checklist. Does the assessment actually contain the evidence rather than commenting on the standard of the evidence?

Mark against criteria: Once you have established the specific criteria for the assessment, ensure you mark against the criteria and not a subjective view as to what you hoped would be there. When using awarding body criteria for assessment, ensure you are marking at the appropriate level. For example, NVQ programmes have specific performance criteria to meet at specific levels. Therefore, you need to mark at the right level for the award.

Use a model answer: Model answers are useful for students and assessors. Students can see what a distinction-level answer is and what a pass-level answer is. It is good practice for learners to 'peer assess' formative assessment pieces and grade also identifying how it could have been improved. This gives learners the opportunity to actively engage with marking criteria and see what evidence should be provided. During standardization activities, assessors can use model answers to grade across a team of assessors, ensuring standards are maintained across marking teams.

Train your assessors: It is important to ensure all markers are trained using set marking criteria. Standardization events help assessors to check their own marking ranges; this is particularly important for new assessors and when awarding body standards change. External moderators/examiners (appointed by the awarding body) regularly check for consistency across a range of markers. It is often more difficult to standardize observational grading; however, programme leaders need to ensure that paired observations (with two assessors) are built into standardization activities.

Validity and reliability

A method of assessment is reliable when individuals, having the same ability, knowledge or skill, achieve the same score or result whenever the method is used and whoever is being assessed (Cotton, 1995).

Is the assessment consistent? Will it work the same way in any place, at any time? (Tummons, 2007).

Methods of assessment

There are a wealth of assessment methods used in education to assess students' achievements, but how to choose? The primary goal is to choose a method which most effectively assesses the objectives of the unit of study or session. In addition, choice of assessment methods should be aligned with the overall aims of the programme and may include the development of other skills (such as critical evaluation or problem solving) and support the development of vocational competencies (such as particular communication or team skills).

When choosing assessment methods, it is useful to have one eye on the immediate task of assessing student learning in a particular unit of study and another eye on the broader aims of the programme and the key core skills of the students.

When considering assessment methods, it is particularly useful to think first about what qualities or abilities you are seeking to underpin. Nightingale et al. (1996) provide eight broad categories of learning outcomes which are listed below. Within each category, some suitable methods are suggested:

Learning outcome	Example tasks
Thinking critically and making judgements (developing arguments, reflecting, evaluating, assessing, judging)	Essay Report Journal Letter of Advice to . . . (about policy, public health matters . . .) Present a case for an interest group Prepare a committee briefing paper for a specific meeting Book review (or article) for a particular journal Write a newspaper article for a foreign newspaper Comment on an article's theoretical perspective
Solving problems and developing plans (identifying problems, posing problems, defining problems, analysing data, reviewing, designing experiments, planning, applying information)	Problem scenario Group work Work-based problem Prepare a report Draft a research bid to a realistic brief Analyse a case study Conference paper (or notes for a conference paper plus annotated bibliography)
Performing procedures and demonstrating techniques (computation, taking readings, using equipment, following laboratory procedures, following protocols, carrying out instructions)	Demonstration Role play Make a video (write script and produce/make a video) Produce a poster Lab report Prepare an illustrated manual on using the equipment, for a particular audience Observation of real or simulated professional practice
Managing and developing self (working cooperatively, working independently, learning independently, being self-directed, managing time, managing tasks, organizing)	Journal Portfolio Learning contract Group work
Accessing and managing information (researching, investigating, interpreting, organizing information, reviewing and paraphrasing information, collecting data, searching and managing information sources, observing and interpreting)	Annotated bibliography Project Dissertation Applied task Applied problem
Demonstrating knowledge and understanding (recalling, describing, reporting, recounting, recognizing, identifying, relating and interrelating)	Written examination Oral examination Essay Report Comment on the accuracy of a set of records Devise an encyclopaedia entry Produce an A to Z of . . . Write an answer to a client's question Short answer questions: True/False/Multiple-Choice Questions (paper-based or computer-aided assessment)

(Continued)

Designing, creating, performing (imagining, visualizing, designing, producing, creating, innovating, performing)	Portfolio
	Performance
	Presentation
	Hypothetical
	Projects
Communicating (one- and two-way communication, commun- ication within a group, verbal, written and nonverbal com- munication. Arguing, describing, advocating, interviewing, negotiating, presenting, using specific written forms)	Written presentation (essay, report, reflective paper etc.)
	Oral presentation
	Group work
	Discussion/debate/role play
	Participate in a 'Court of Enquiry'
	Presentation to camera
	Observation of real or simulated professional practice

Variety in assessment

It is interesting to note that the above eight assessment areas would be what we would like to see all our students achieving (at different levels) according to the programme of study they are taking. However, when choosing assessment methods we tend to stick to the 'tried and tested' methods of essay writing and academic tests/exams as these were the methods that we were tested with. When choosing methods, it is important to offer variety to learners in the way they demonstrate their learning and to help them develop a well-rounded set of abilities by the time they achieve the award.

> When we do assessment we essentially ask the following:
> What do the educational experiences of our students add up to?
> Can our students integrate learning from individual courses into a coherent whole?
> Do our students have the knowledge, skills and values a graduate should possess?
> How can student learning be improved?

The quality of assessment practice may be improved as follows:

> integrating assessment into schemes of work;
> planning assessment to reinforce learning as well as measure it;
> using methods that allow learners to show what they know, understand and can do;
> responding to diversity and providing additional support where needed;
> making sure that methods used for formative assessment contribute to learning and prepare learners for forms of assessment they will encounter at the summative stage or in programmes to which they hope to progress;
> sharing good practice in assessment, developing common approaches within programmes and moderating outcomes;
> recognizing that assessment cannot capture all of the learning that takes place and being clear what is to be assessed, how and why (Excellence gateway, 2009).

Linking to the first chapter on initial assessment, tutors need to ensure that all learners undergo initial and diagnostic assessment. This is to ensure that learners are on the right programme at the right level and that, if necessary, they receive support in functional skills. Tutors also need to ensure that planned learning styles are appropriate to individual learners (also discussed in Chapter 1).

Black and William's review of assessment

Conventional practice – 'Teach, test, grade and move on' (assessment is summative)

Best practice – 'Find faults, fix and follow up' (assessment is diagnostic)

Mastery learning

Mastery Learning is a teaching strategy method that presumes all students can learn if they are provided with the appropriate learning conditions. It is a method whereby students are not moved on to a subsequent learning objective until they demonstrate competency with the current one. Mastery learning generally consists of specific topics which all students begin together. Students who are not yet competent at a topic are given additional instruction until they succeed. Students who master the topic early engage in extension activities until the entire group can progress together. Mastery learning includes many elements of successful tutoring and continual assessment. In this learning environment, the teacher directs a variety of group-based teaching strategies, with frequent and specific feedback by using diagnostic, formative testing as well as regularly correcting mistakes students make along their learning path.

The essence of mastery learning strategies is group instruction supplemented by frequent feedback and individually corrective help as each student needs it (Bloom, Madaus and Hastings, 1981).

There are five stages in Mastery Learning:

Mastery objectives defined.

Give the assessment criteria and carry out formative assessment.

Set tests that are short, frequent and self-assessed.

Students who pass get a P for pass; nothing is recorded for those who did not pass.

Students who did not pass look carefully at the feedback and then try the test again.

Action planning and reflective practice

Following on from Chapter 1, where we looked at the importance of individual learning plans not only for your students but also to be used throughout your teacher training programme, your own ILP should be updated throughout your training through reflective practice and action planning. The importance of reflecting on what you are doing, as part of the learning process, has been emphasized by many investigators.

Kolb (1984) provides one of the most useful descriptive models available of the adult learning process and experiential learning. The suggestion is that there are four stages in learning which follow from each other: *Concrete Experience* is followed by *Reflection* on that experience on a personal basis. This may then be followed by describing the experience, or the application of known theories to it (*Abstract Conceptualisation*), and hence to the construction of ways of modifying the next occurrence of the experience (*Active Experimentation*), leading in turn to the next *Concrete Experience*. Honey and Mumford (1982) have built on Kolb's theory, developing Learning Styles around this sequence (see Chapter 1 on learning styles) and identifying individual preferences for each stage (Activist, Reflector, Theorist and Pragmatist, respectively). Not all forms of skill and knowledge emphasize all the stages of the Cycle to the same extent, and Kolb has carried the argument further by relating topics and subject areas to the cycle in the following ways:

Concrete Experience corresponds to 'knowledge by acquaintance', direct practical experience (or 'Apprehension' in Kolb's terms), as opposed to 'knowledge about' something, which is theoretical, but perhaps more comprehensive (hence 'Comprehension') and represented by *Abstract Conceptualisation*.

Reflective Observation concentrates on what the experience means to the 'experiencer' (it is transformed by 'Intension') or its *connotations*, while *Active Experimentation* transforms the theory of Abstract Conceptualisation by testing it in practice (by 'Extension') and relates to its *denotations* (Atherton, 2009).

The Institute for Learning (IfL)

The IfL is the professional body for teachers, trainers and assessor across further education (FE), including adult and community learning, emergency and public services, FE colleges, the armed services, the voluntary sector and work-based learning. In 2002, IfL was incorporated as an independent professional body limited to FE, at the time. A Transitional Council was formed, and the process of attracting a volunteer paying membership began. Also in 2002 the government publishes *Success for All*, a reform agenda for the learning and skills sector. In 2004, IfL's prospects of becoming a fully established professional body was influenced by the seminal DFES policy document, *Equipping Our Teachers for the Future*. Policy makers recognize that, through the IfL's growing voluntary membership, it has an 'influential voice as the professional body representing teachers in the sector' and identify its central role in the reform of initial teacher training for new entrants to the sector. In recognition of the reach of *Equipping Our Teachers for the Future* beyond FE colleges to the wider Learning and Skills Council (LSC)-funded sector, the IfL has renamed itself as the Institute for Learning (Post Compulsory Education and Training). In 2010, the IfL was recognized as the professional body for teacher professionalism and maintained a register of practising teachers in the sector. The IfL's work is driven by a commitment to promote value and develop the professionalism of members. A key priority is to support individual teachers' and trainers' learning so that they can maintain their high professional status and have long-term continuing professional development (CPD) interests as career teachers.

> The role of IfL as the professional body for trainers, tutors and student teachers in the Lifelong Learning Sector is to
> raise the status of teaching practitioners in the sector,
> develop a model of teacher professionalism which captures and articulates the dual role of teachers as both subject specialists and professional teachers,
> have all Registered Teachers IfL members and therefore subject to their Code of Professional Practice and the associated disciplinary processes,
> ensure teachers employed before September 2007 are registered with IfL for CPD monitoring,
> ensure teachers employed after September 2007 register with IfL and successfully complete the professional formation process to become Licensed Practitioners *(QTLS)*.

Regulations state that staff in a teaching role who deliver teaching and learning through LSC provision must be members of the IFL. This includes teachers, tutors, trainers, lecturers, instructors and anyone teaching as part of their role regardless of job title, type of contract (full- or part-time) or whether they combine teaching with other non-teaching-related roles. (This includes agency staff.)

Staff teaching solely in Higher Education are not required by the regulations to register with IfL, but it is a requirement of the College to maintain a CPD Log. Staff who are not considered teachers under the requirements are people in purely non-teaching roles, such as assessors (non-teaching), verifiers (non-teaching) and learning support practitioners.

The IfL has identified the requirements from September 2007 that teachers will be required to register with the IfL. This must be done on an annual basis (in the future from 1 April each year). The newly appointed teachers, from September 2007, must register within six months of appointment.

The ideal requirement is for full-time staff to complete 30 hours of CPD during each academic year.

Pro-rata reductions of the minimum requirements for CPD will apply in relation to absence on account of statutory maternity, paternal, paternity or adoption leave or on account of certified long-term absence of more than three months.

All forms of professional development, accredited or non-accredited, will be valued and recognized within a minimum annual tariff of 30 hours.

Teachers will be expected to summarize their professional and occupational development in a record of their CPD, reflecting on the impact made on their professional practice including improvements in teaching and supporting learning.

Teachers are required to make their CPD record available to IfL and the College for inspection. (IfL began sampling from the start of 2009.) All staff are encouraged to use the College's CPD Log on the self-service option of the HR/Payroll system to maintain their own CPD Log.

There is a requirement for management staff who are also contracted to teach to undertake CPD and register with the IfL.

Licensed practitioner
Qualified Teacher Learning and Skills (QTLS) – Full
Associate Teacher Learning and Skills (ATLS) – Associate

This will be conferred by the IfL upon the successful completion of professional formation. This process of workplace assessment is not expected to be time related; rather it will be based upon employer evaluation and referral. The process of becoming a Licensed Practitioner will be confirmed by the Institute once the Regulations are in place.

The license will be annually renewable, including a CPD obligation, and can be withdrawn or suspended subject to the outcome of an investigation of alleged misconduct. On 1st June 2007, Bill Rammell MP, Minister of State for Lifelong Learning, Further and Higher Education, stated,

> . . . there has been widespread support in FE for us to introduce requirements for teachers to undertake continuing professional development and become professionally registered with the Institute for Learning. I am, therefore, pleased to announce today that this Government will meet the full costs of the professional registration with the IfL. Such an investment supports our aim of professionalising the FE workforce, while registration will ensure that teachers are qualified and complete at least 30 hours of continuing professional development per year. (www.ifl.ac.uk, accessed 8th June 2010)

Definition of CPD

CPD means maintaining, improving and broadening relevant knowledge and skills in your subject specialism and your teaching so that it has a positive impact on practice and learner experience. *Equipping our Teachers for the Future* introduced the requirement to 'remain in good standing' to maintain the Licence to Practise. All teachers will be required to demonstrate evidence of post-qualification professional development and to comply with a Code of Professional Practice. It can be argued that CPD is most effective when teachers reflect on their professional practice, develop a plan based on their identified needs and match this to the context of their employment, organizational context and development plan. CPD should link professional development relating to subject specialism to teaching and learning and lead to improvement in professional practice.

The IfL code of practice 2008 identifies useful criteria when thinking of engaging in CPD. The code of practice states the following:

> A growing body of research on CPD has shown that the kinds of professional development which make the most difference to practice are based on professional dialogue about teaching and learning, and the improvement of practice through a variety of activities, including coaching, mentoring, shadowing and peer support. Awareness-raising events are useful for absorbing information and updating knowledge, but are not likely to lead to skills development. Therefore, when deciding on

your priorities for CPD, it is important to consider what kinds of CPD will be the most effective for developing your practice as a teacher. (www.ifl.ac.uk, accessed 8th June 2010)

The IfL go on to say that you will need to show, year on year, that you are improving the relevant knowledge and skills in your area of subject expertise and in your teaching or training. In this sense, CPD is personalized and any activities that are undertaken for the purposes of keeping up to date with the latest developments in a subject area and keeping abreast of changes in teaching methods will count as meaningful professional development, as long as these questions can be answered:

What professional development activities have you undertaken this year?
Have you reflected on the learning you have gained from these activities?
Have the activities and the reflection made a difference to how you teach or train?
Can you show evidence of what the difference is and the impact it has made to learners, colleagues or the organization in which you work?

Your record of CPD for any one year needs to show that as a self-regulating professional you can demonstrate reflection, improvement and positive impact, and these will all be personal to you and the context in which you practise as a teacher and trainer.

The IfL have suggested that there ought to be a minimum of 30-hours CPD per year for a full-time teacher; however, they also suggest appropriate number of hours for part-time teachers/trainers. As a guide they suggest,

Average teaching CPD hours	Hours per week
0–4	6
5–8	10
9–12	14
13–16	18
17–20	22
21–23	26
24+	30

When deciding on the most appropriate CPD activities, it is good to consider the overarching standards for teachers/trainers produced by Lifelong Learning UK (LLUK); these are the standards that are used at the end of each chapter in this book. Using these standards will ideally help you to choose specific areas for development and teaching and learning skill development. Some of the skills you could try to update or engage with could include the following:

peer coaching (coaching others and being coached in your subject or vocational area);
subject learning coach or advanced learning coach training;

mentoring new colleagues;

peer review;

peer observation;

work shadowing;

team teaching;

leading team/department self-assessment;

carrying out and disseminating action research;

designing innovative feedback mechanisms (learners and peers);

chairing team meetings;

constructing professional dialogue/learning conversation opportunities – for more ideas visit *www.gtce.org.uk*;

becoming an e-CPD adviser or e-guide;

being an active member of a committee, board or steering groups related to teaching and/or your subject area;

peer visits to community organizations/partners;

curriculum design/development/validation;

reading and reviewing books or journal articles;

updating knowledge through the internet/TV (including teachers' TV), other media and reviewing these with a group of professional colleagues;

sharing idea and resources with other teachers and trainers through REfLECT (IfL's CPD electronic recording system).

IfL's six-step approach to reflecting on your CPD experience
Step 1 – contextual analysis

If you are a new teacher or trainer (from September 2007), your priority is to become qualified and gain QTLS or ATLS. If you are already qualified, you will need to begin reflection on the relationship between LLUK standards for teachers and the development of your professional practice (visit www. lluk.org for further details). Use the model of dual professionalism and think about the context in which you work, what the key priorities are for keeping up to date in your subject area and in your approaches to teaching and training.

Step 2 – needs and goals analysis

Analyse your priority areas using appropriate forms of evidence, such as learner feedback, impact evaluation, employer appraisals and teaching observations. Also make a critical self-assessment of your needs and goals for the coming year that will address identified areas for development.

Step 3 – individual development plan

Using the evidence from this self-assessment, identify professional development activities that you think will address your needs thinking carefully about the type of activity as well as the focus or topics that are most likely to be effective for you. Create a professional development plan giving:

⇨

a brief rationale for each activity,
a timeline for achievement,
outcomes and
what you think will be the measures of success.

Step 4 – professional development log

Carry out the activities identified in your plan, keep an account of the activities you complete with dates and some indication of the time spent together with your reflections on progress and the difference the activities are making to you, colleagues and learners.

Step 5 – professional development record

You will probably accumulate many more hours than the 30 (or pro-rata) that are required, but towards the end of the cycle put together the most significant activities that have made the most impact on your practice in a record of professional development. This will evidence that you have completed the required number of hours of CPD for your teaching or training role and crucially will also show the impact of what you have achieved.

Step 6 – reflection on practice and impact analysis

Reflect on the impact on your professional practice, and on your colleagues and learners, of each aspect of CPD you have undertaken. This will be one of the prompts for the next cycle and will also be an integral part of your learning log for the current year (www.ifl.ac.uk, 2009).

Regulatory bodies such as IfL and LLUK identify CPD as a prominent aspect of keeping your skills and knowledge as a professional teacher/trainer up to date. Education organizations recognize the benefits of investing in staff CPD to improve student retention. CPD can also be defined as the conscious updating of professional knowledge and the improvement of professional competence throughout a person's working life. It is a commitment to being professional, keeping up to date and continuously seeking to improve. It is one of the key factors involved in optimizing your career opportunities, both today and for the future. Good professional development is an investment worth making and one we need to make if we are to realize our goal of providing high quality education (IPD, 2000, www.ipd.org.uk, accessed 8 June 2010).

Linking to action planning

Following on from the previous chapter, PTLLS, you should regularly review and update your action plan. Have you achieved the targets you set? If yes, then you need to set new targets and achievement dates; if no, then you will need to revisit this target and analyse the reasons for non-completion. It is important to ask whether your working/learning environment has changed and whether this is hindering the completion of this target. Did you plan insufficient time for completion? Does this target still need to be achieved or has the working towards completion actually changed the need?

You may be able to look at the strengths, weaknesses, opportunities and challenges (SWOC) analysis technique again to revise the focus of your development. Talk through this with your tutor, mentor or a colleague. An example is shown below:

Action planning update
Academic SWOC analysis

Complete this analysis as you complete the module following on from PTLLS. (Consider your study skills, academic writing, Harvard referencing, literacy, numeracy, ICT, Equality and Diversity when planning, designing and delivering lessons; teaching skills; Mentorship and tuition.) Be specific especially with the Literacy and numeracy developments, look back at your diagnostic report and identify where you still need to improve.

Strengths	Weaknesses
Opportunities	Challenges

Once you have identified your SWOC, you can use this information to update your formal action plan. Ensure you discuss this with your tutor/mentor or colleague.

The following action plan has been discussed and agreed by:

Tutor name: Student name:
Signature: Signature:
Date:

Action plan

(Consider your study skills, academic writing, Harvard referencing, literacy, numeracy, ICT, Equality and Diversity when planning, designing and delivering lessons; teaching skills; Mentorship and tuition)

Aim	Method of Achievement	Time-scale	Evidence of Achievement

Summary of key points

In this chapter, we have looked at the differences between different teaching and learning strategies. We have highlighted the advantages and disadvantages of these strategies and linked these to teacher- and student-centred learning. The section on assessment discusses the range of assessment methods available. This section also identifies why we assess learners and why motivational assessment and feedback to learners is important for success. The final section of the chapter looks at reflective practice and links to continuous professional development by focusing on meeting the IfL's requirements for annual CPD using this information to inform personal action planning. It can be suggested that the teaching process involves a number of different skills and qualities. As well as the initial delivery of content, it is important to ensure that student learning is reinforced by appropriate assessment. This assessment may be formative and summative. Teaching is not a profession that should necessarily be 'difficult'. Learning and teaching can be an inspiring process, but for this to occur it is important to reflect on experience in order to develop innovative practice.

This chapter links to the following LLUK professional standards:

Professional values

AS 4: Reflection and evaluation of their own practice and their CPD as teachers.

AS 7: Improving the quality of their practice.

BS 1: Maintaining an inclusive, equitable and motivating learning environment.

BS 2: Applying and developing own professional skills to enable learners to achieve their goals.

CS 1: Understanding and keeping up to date with current knowledge in respect of own specialist area.

CS 2: Enthusing and motivating learners in own specialist area.

CS 3: Fulfilling the statutory responsibilities associated with own specialist area of teaching.

CS 4: Developing good practice in teaching own specialist area.

DS 3: Evaluation of own effectiveness in planning learning.

ES 1: Designing and using assessment as a tool for learning and progression.

ES 2: Assessing the work of learners in a fair and equitable manner.

ES 3: Learner involvement and shared responsibility in the assessment process.

ES 4: Using feedback as a tool for learning and progression.

Professional knowledge and understanding

AK 1.1: What motivates learners to learn and the importance of learners' experience and aspirations.

AK 3.1: Issues of equality, diversity and inclusion.

AK 4.2: The impact of own practice on individuals and their learning.

AK 4.3: Ways to reflect, evaluate and use research to develop own practice and to share good practice with others.

AK 6.1: Relevant statutory requirements and codes of practice.

BK 1.3: Ways of creating a motivating learning environment.

BK 2.2: Ways to engage, motivate and encourage active participation of learners and learner independence.

BK 2.7: Ways in which mentoring and/or coaching can support the development of professional skills and knowledge.

BK 3.3: Ways to structure and present information and ideas clearly and effectively to learners.

CK 1.1: Own specialist area including current developments.

CK 3.1: Teaching and learning theories and strategies relevant to own specialist area.

⇨

EK 1.1: Theories and principles of assessment and the application of different forms of assessment, including initial, formative and summative assessment in teaching and learning.

EK 1.2: Ways to devise, select, use and appraise assessment tools, including, where appropriate, those which exploit new and emerging technologies.

EK 3.1: Ways to establish learner involvement in and personal responsibility for assessment of their learning.

EK 3.2: Ways to ensure access to assessment within a learning programme.

Professional practice

AP 4.2: Reflect on and demonstrate commitment to improvement of own personal and teaching skills through regular evaluation and use of feedback.

AP 4.3: Share good practice with others and engage in CPD through reflection, evaluation and appropriate use of research.

AP 7.3: Use feedback to develop own practice within the organization's systems.

BP 1.3: Create a motivating environment which encourages learners to reflect on, evaluate and make decisions about their learning.

BP 2.2: Use a range of effective and appropriate teaching and learning techniques to engage and motivate learners and encourage independence.

BP 2.3: Implement learning activities which develop the skills and approaches of all learners and promote learner autonomy.

BP 2.4: Apply flexible and varied delivery methods as appropriate

EP 1.2: Devise, select, use and appraise assessment tools, including, where appropriate, those which exploit new and emerging technologies.

EP 2.1: Apply appropriate methods of assessment fairly and effectively.

EP 2.2: Apply appropriate assessment methods to produce valid, reliable and sufficient evidence.

Self-assessment questions

Question 1: Name two student-centred teaching strategies.
Question 2: What are the benefits of student-centred learning for the learner?
Question 3: What should we consider when giving feedback to learners following assessment?

Moving on feature

This chapter has looked at the different range of teaching and learning strategies available to us and how these strategies can be more student centred. We have also looked in detail about assessment and the different forms of assessment. The next chapter explores the theories and principles that inform teaching in relation to planning and enabling learning and assessment. The chapter reviews theories and principles of learning, assessment and communication to enable student teachers to evaluate and improve own communication skills.

Further Reading

Petty, G. (2004), *Teaching Today* (3rd Edition). Cheltenham: Nelson Thornes.

Fawbert, F. (2003), *Teaching in Post-Compulsory Education: Learning, Skills and Standards.* London: Continuum.

Mariani, L. (1996) *Brain-Dominance Questionnaire* [on-line]. Available: http://www.scs.sk.ca/cyber/Present/brain Accessed: 16 March 2010.

Reece, I. and Walker, S. (2007), *Teaching Training and Learning: A Practical Guide.* Sunderland: Business Education Publishers.

Wallace, S. (2007), *Teaching Tutoring and Training in the Lifelong Learning Sector.* Exeter: Learning Matters.

An excellent textbook that is written in an accessible way and makes clear links to applying theory to practice.

Tummons, J. (2007), *Becoming a Professional Tutor in the Lifelong Learning Sector.* Exeter: Learning Matters.

A very useful and interesting text which is current and explores key issues surrounding being a professional in the Lifelong Learning Sector.

References

Armitage, A. et al. (1999), *Teaching and Training in Post-Compulsory Education.* Buckingham: Open University Press.

Atherton, J. S. (2009), *Learning and Teaching; Experiential Learning* [Online]. Available: http://www.learningandteaching.info/learning/experience.htm Accessed: 15 January 2010.

Bloom, B. S., Madaus, G. F. and Hastings, J. T. (1981), *Evaluation to Improve Learning.* New York and London: McGraw-Hill.

Cotton, K. (1995), *Effective Schooling Practices: A Research Synthesis.* Portland, OR: Regional Educational Laboratory.

Hermann, N. (1982), *The Creative Brain.* New York: Nedd Hermann Group.

Hebditch, M. (1990) cited in Petty, G. (1998) *Teaching Today* (2nd Edition). Cheltenham: Nelson Thornes.

Honey, P. and Mumford, A. (1982), *The Manual of Learning Styles.* Maidenhead: Peter Honey.

IfL Code of Professional Practice, 1 April 2008, Institute for Learning Publication.

Kolb, D. A. (1984), *Experiential Learning.* Englewood Cliffs: Prentice-Hall.

McLean, J. (1997), *Flexible Learning and the Learning Organisation.* MSc Management Dissertation: Staffordshire University.

Nightingale, P., Te Wiata, I. T., Toohey, S., Ryan, G., Hughes, C. and Magin, D. (1996), *Assessing Learning in Universities.* Australia: Professional Development Centre, University of New South Wales.

Petty, G. (1998), *Teaching Today* (2nd Edition). Cheltenham: Nelson Thornes.

Rogers, C. (1969). *Freedom to Learn.* New York: Merrill.

Tummons, J. (2007), *Becoming a Professional Tutor in the Lifelong Learning Sector.* Exeter: Learning Matters.

Electronic references

Educational Initiative Centre (2004), sited in www.direct.gov.uk

Excellence gateway (2009), Learning and Skills Improvement Service online: www.excellencegateway.org.uk

Institute for Learning (2010), www.ifl.ac.uk

International Professional Development Association, 2010, www.ipda.org.uk

Oxford Dictionary online: www.askoxford.com

Theories and Principles for Planning and Enabling Learning and Assessment

Learning Outcomes

After reading this chapter you should be able to

apply theories of learning (behaviourism, cognitivism and humanism) to planning learning;
use Bloom's taxonomies of learning to create effective, differentiated learning outcomes;
identify key strategies for good communication in the classroom.

Introduction

This chapter links with Chapter 4 where we discuss learning theories and their application to education and the classroom. It is hoped you will be able to use this information to link your curriculum and lesson planning to key learning theories. This skill will ensure you are fully aware of the learning experiences your learners are engaging with and therefore help your planning skills to improve.

Clear understanding of Bloom's taxonomies will help you to build on the work we have already covered in Chapter 1, identifying the need for clear, differentiated learning outcomes which are set at different levels to offer challenge to your learners.

The final section in this chapter focuses on communication skills. Effective communication skills are essential for all teachers; however, we must also look at the development of our learners' communications skills to develop core functional skills for the workplace.

Educational psychology

Educational psychology is the study of how humans learn in educational settings, the effectiveness of educational interventions, the psychology of teaching and the social psychology of schools as organizations. Educational psychology is concerned with how students learn and develop. Educational psychology can in part be understood through its relationship with other disciplines. It in turn informs a wide range of specialties within educational studies, including planning learning, educational technology, curriculum development, education for students with learning difficulties and disabilities and classroom management.

Using educational psychology, this section defines and contrasts the types of behavioural learning theories – learning by association (classical and operant conditioning); it also describes cognitive and humanistic theories, giving examples of how each can be used in the classroom.

Theories of learning: Behaviourism

According to the behaviourists, learning can be defined as *the relatively permanent change in behaviour brought about as a result of experience or practice.* Behaviourists recognize that learning is an internal event. However, it is not recognized as learning until it is displayed by overt behaviour.

Learning by association: The term 'learning theory' is often associated with the behavioural view. The focus of the behavioural approach is on how the environment impacts overt behaviour. Remember that biological maturation or genetics is an alternative explanation for relatively permanent change.

We are so used to seeing trade marks in the media and around our environment. The trade marks for Mercedes-Benz, Nike and McDonalds, for example, are so familiar that we do not need the company name to recognize who they are. This is because we have learnt the company name through association. We now associate the logo/picture with the organization. How many more pictures do you see on a daily basis that you do not need an explanation or title to recognize?

Advertising plays a vital role in conditioning us. The media and marketing groups pair a stimulus (the product) with a conditioned response. This means that a new car (a neutral stimulus) is associated with a positive conditioned stimulus (models, fun, sex etc.). Summer holidays are advertised with good weather, lovely beaches, nice hotels and the image of having a good time. The reverse can also happen, in other words, creating negative associations such as in political advertising (pairing something unpleasant with a particular party).

Education and learning by association examples

Students learn a particular subject because they unconsciously associate it with a teacher they like.

In class to end group discussions the teacher always stands in a particular spot every time; students will learn what this means.

Learning through use of mnemonics – associating a difficult spelling perhaps with a phrase or sentence; i.e., to learn to spell the word *science*, it could be broken down to 'Science Can Interest Every Nosy Child Everywhere'.

Classical conditioning theory

Classical conditioning was the first type of learning to be discovered and studied within the behaviourist tradition (hence the name classical).

The major theorist in the development of classical conditioning is Ivan Pavlov, a Russian scientist trained in biology and medicine (as was his German contemporary, Sigmund Freud). Pavlov was studying the digestive system of dogs and became intrigued with his observation that dogs deprived of food began to salivate when one of his assistants walked into the room. He began to investigate this phenomenon and established the laws of classical conditioning.

During his investigations, he discovered that an unconditioned stimulus (US) will naturally (without learning) elicit or bring about a reflexive response. His studies with dogs showed before a neutral stimulus was added to the experiment a natural response would occur to the US. However, over time the US paired with the neutral stimulus elicits an unconditioned response (UR), finally resulting in the conditioned stimulus producing a conditioned response, as Figure 3.1 shows.

Applied to the classroom, classical conditioning is seen primarily in the conditioning of emotional behaviour. Things that make us happy, sad, angry, become associated with neutral stimuli that gain our attention. For example, the school, classroom, teacher or subject matter are initially neutral stimuli that gain attention. Activities at school or in the classroom automatically elicit emotional responses, and these activities are associated with the neutral or

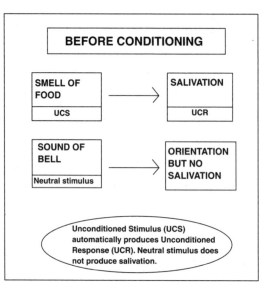

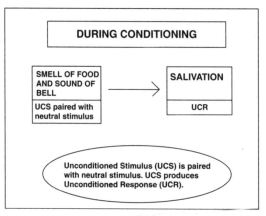

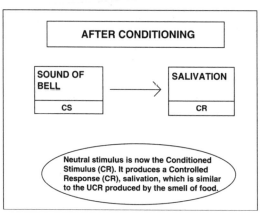

Figure 3.1 Classical conditioning Source: Based on Huitt and Hummel (1999).

orienting stimulus. After repeated presentations, the previously neutral response will elicit the emotional response. The following is an example:

> Student is bullied at school.
> Student feels bad when bullied.
> Student associates being bullied and school.
> Student begins to feel bad when she thinks of school.

In order to extinguish the associated of feeling bad and thinking of school, the connection between school and being bullied must be broken.

Operant conditioning

Operant conditioning is a type of learning in which behaviour is strengthened when followed by a reinforcer (reward) or diminished if followed by a punishment. Operant behaviour operates on the environment, producing consequences.

It is important to distinguish between the who and the what is being reinforced, punished or extinguished; it is the response that is reinforced, punished or extinguished, not the person. In addition, reinforcement, punishment and extinction are not terms restricted to the laboratory. Naturally occurring consequences can also be said to reinforce, punish or extinguish behaviour and are not always delivered by people.

Reinforcement is a consequence that causes a behaviour to occur with greater frequency or a behaviour that is to be encouraged. Punishment is a consequence that causes a behaviour to occur with less frequency; the behaviour is inappropriate and not to be repeated. Extinction is the lack of any consequence following a behaviour. When a behaviour is inconsequential, producing neither favourable nor unfavourable consequences, it will occur with less frequency. When a previously reinforced behaviour is no longer reinforced with either positive or negative reinforcement, it leads to a decline in the response.

The major theorist in the development of operant conditioning is Burrhus F. Skinner (1904-1990). Skinner believed that internal thoughts and motivations could not be used to explain behaviour. Instead, he suggested, we should look only at the external, observable causes of human behaviour.

Skinner's box

In operant conditioning, the subject's behaviours are reinforced by desirable results, punished by undesirable results or extinguished by having no result. Reinforced behaviours will occur more frequently, while punished and extinguished behaviours will be performed less often. An example of operant conditioning is a rat learning to navigate a maze more quickly and efficiently after a number of attempts.

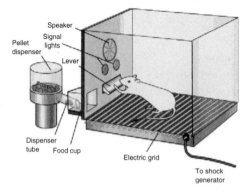

Figure 3.2 Skinner and operant learning

Note: Skinner defined operant learning as (a) voluntary and goal directed and (b) controlled by its consequences—strengthened if rewarded or weakened if punished.

The mouse is "operating" on its environment by pressing the food lever in the Skinner box and receiving a food reward.

A Skinner box, used to study these concepts, is a box that houses an animal and offers both unconditioned and conditioned stimuli – such as coloured lights and food, respectively – and response levers or keys that serve to monitor the animal's behaviour. For example, a Skinner box may be used to test classical conditioning in a bird by associating a red light with each feeding, eventually causing the bird to peck not only at food but upon seeing the red light. A Skinner box may be fairly simple, with only one lever or key, or it may be quite complex, with a variety of stimuli and ways of monitoring response. The Skinner box has received criticism because it does not capture every aspect of the animal's behaviour; pushing the lever with a nose or a paw registers as the same response, for example, and light touches of the lever may not be recorded (Figure 3.2 is from Huitt & Hummel [1999]).

Applications of operant conditioning

Superstitious behaviour: Superstitions that are reinforced can have a similar effect; in other words, some people believe it is dangerous to walk under a ladder. If they attempt to walk under a ladder and a negative response occurs (for example, they trip and fall), their superstition will become stronger; however, if they walk under a ladder and then win the lottery, the superstition will no longer have the same negative response.

Behaviour management: We can use a 'punishment' to manage classroom behaviour; for example, if a student is constantly late for class, you may want to use a negative reinforcement, i.e. no break or missing ten minutes of their lunch time. If this strategy is adhered to for all learners' lateness, the inappropriate behaviour would decrease. (See Chapter 4 for more examples.)

What aspects of education are behaviourist?

Teach by shaping desired behaviour – rewards and punishments
Being a role model by personifying appropriate behaviour
Tests – often involve memory (remember the mnemonics)
Step-by-step approach
Break big tasks into bite-size tasks, allows for frequent experience of success
Quick feedback: motivational
Demonstrations are important
Allow learners to practice
Operant conditioning overview

If a behaviour is reinforced, it is more likely to be repeated. Reinforcement must follow the desired behaviour as soon as possible, and consistency and sticking to the programme are essential to success. Behaviour is shaped into the desired behaviour by using 'successive approximations'. Variable Ratio is the most powerful method of reinforcement for maintaining behaviour, as seen by addiction to one-arm bandits and playing the lottery.

Positive reinforcement

We reinforce in a variety of ways, for example, verbal (praise), good grades, nonverbal cues (head nodding, smiling, raising eyebrows etc.).

Negative reinforcement

Incentives – e.g. if you pass all of the assignments during the term, you do not have to take the end-of-term exam.

Punishment

Should be used sparingly, as the student is not learning what *to* do but rather what *not* to do.

Teaching activities

Skills drills (repetitive exercises)	Worksheets
Programmed instruction	Memorization
Role play (realistic practice)	Modelling
Multiple-choice questions	Practice
Step-by-step approach	Teacher talk
Token economies	

Applying in the classroom

Students remember what they experience frequently.
Stress key points: Summarize at the beginning and end of classes.
Praise and encourage (past success provides motivation for present learning).

Set clear objectives and use these to measure students' achievement.
Allow time for practice, not just theory.

Criticisms of the approach

Teacher led/centred
Passive view of learners
Authoritarian
External reinforcement is used to motivate learners
Structured process
Removes learners freedom

Cognitive learning theory

Activity 3.1

Think of a number between 1 and 10.
Double the number.
Add 8.
Half the number.
Subtract the original number from the new number.
Give the number a letter: 'A' for 1, 'B' for 2, 'C' for 3, 'D' for 4, 'E' for 5 etc.
Think of a European country that begins with the letter.
Think of an animal you might see in a circus that begins with the second letter of the European country!
(Answer is given below.)

Cognitive theory is based on the premise that there are thought processes behind the behaviour. It began with Gestalt theories of perception; interested in the way the brain imposes pattern on the perceived world, Gestalt moved into problem-solving learning. It is also much influenced by the developmental psychology of Piaget, focusing on the maturational factors affecting understanding. The accommodation/assimilation dialectic is the part most useful for understanding grown learners. Broadly, cognitive theory is interested in how people understand material and thus aptitude and capacity to learn and learning styles (discussed in Chapters 1 and 2). It is also the basis of the educational approach known as constructivism, which emphasizes the role of the learner in constructing his own view or model of the material and what helps with that.

Answer to activity

Were your answers Denmark and Elephant? This is because you have already learnt that Denmark is a European country beginning with D and Elephant is perhaps one of the few zoo animals beginning with E. You have used your cognitive memory skills to identify the answers.

Memory

Memory is a very complex topic, much researched and at the heart of the cognitive theory. Memory is central to learning, which could not happen without it: Indeed, 'memorizing' is a synonym for the lowest levels of rote learning. Memorizing begins with a sensory buffer; this is only a part of memory information and may stay there for about 1/15th of a second, while the brain assembles it to 'make sense'. We are familiar with the illusion by which a succession of still pictures presented rapidly enough appears to be moving: It is the basis of all cinematography. Once the frame rate drops below about 16 frames per second, however, we may well become conscious of the flicker or jumps from one still image to another. Similarly, we do not hear a succession of speech sounds but complete words or phrases: It is as if the brain waits to assemble a meaningful sound before passing it on to the next stage, which is Short-Term Memory (STM). Research suggests that STM deals best with sounds rather than visual stimuli, but that may perhaps be due to the fact that visual stimuli are taken in all at once, whereas sounds are processed in a linear fashion—over time. In any event, the STM holds material for about 15-30 seconds, although this can be expanded by practice. This is much shorter than most of us think—a lot of people seem to think that it lasts for ten minutes or so. The STM has a capacity of seven items (plus or minus two). However, 'items' are defined by meaning rather than size, so it may be difficult to remember telephone numbers of more than seven digits, but if '01234' is remembered as 'Teesside STD code' it becomes just one item, and remembering '7,9,3,1,5,6' after it becomes simpler. If that too is 'chunked' as 'my work phone number' it is even easier. This, of course, assumes that a label for the 'chunk' already exists in long-term memory (LTM).

Theoretically, LTM has infinite capacity and lasts for the rest of your life. Tulving (1985) suggested the useful distinction between three components of LTM:

Semantic memory stores concepts and ideas.

Episodic (sometimes referred to as 'autobiographical' or 'narrative') memory contains memories of events.

Procedural memory concerns skills and 'know-how' rather than 'know-that' knowledge.

People with amnesia, for example, typically lose episodic memory, but other memories may be relatively intact. Episodic and semantic memory are more prone to distortion than procedural memory, which is more robust: A skill lost through lack of practice typically comes back rapidly when called upon and without significant degradation. However, semantic and episodic memories are more amenable to linguistic description and communication (adapted from Atherton, 2009).

Memory is a problem of data storage and retrieval. We cannot remember everything which can be frustrating (for example, exams). Like attention, it is impossible to deal with all the information we receive. Efficient memory relies on forgetting most things but remembering the important stuff. Memory is linked to learning and is affected by a number of things:

Practice: The more times a piece of information is encountered, the more likely you are to remember it, the more likely it is to be committed to LTM.

Stage theory: Information passes through STM on its way to LTM.

Primacy: The first thing in a list is remembered well.

Recency/retention: The last thing encountered is remembered well.

Activity 3.2

How can you read this?

How can you raed tihs pciee of inofmtoin wehn the wrdos are all jmumbeld up?

Is tiher a paettren?

Can you sopt it?

Feedback

When the first and last letters of a word stay the same but the letters in the middle of the word are jumbled up, the brain can still perceive the word that it has learnt, by building up from previous knowledge and LTM.

Memory involves encoding, storage and retrieval, but you cannot have retrieval without going through the process of encoding and storing.

Cognitive applications

Cognitive strategies are still teacher led, but learning is far more active for the learners. They are more involved in lessons and are given tasks, e.g. problem solving. Gestalt's principles suggest the following: Learners should be encouraged to discover the underlying nature of a topic or problem (i.e. the relationship). Instruction should be based on the laws of organization, i.e. clear planning with learners organizing the new learning by application to the old.

The cognitivistic approach is an academic approach based on the principles that learning occurs primarily through exposure to logically presented information. A good analogy is having two pails. Picture the full pail of the wise teacher pouring its contents into the empty pail of the less informed learner. Cognitivism is the 'tell' approach to learning; its predominant learning activity is the lecture. Current trends, however, run to shorter, mini-lectures geared to a 'PlayStation', multi-media culture. Cognitive techniques used in the classroom are as follows:

Diagrams

Films

Panels

Interviews with subject specialists

Class presentations
Readings
Debates
Case studies

Some of the advantages to using a cognitive curriculum or approach include building on a base of knowledge to extend learners knowledge or information on concepts and rules. It can provide the rationale upon which the learner can build action; it is seen as faster than behaviourist or humanist methods and therefore does not waste time and learners feel they are treated as adults.

Cognitive applications to the classroom

Information should be presented logically.
Treating people like adults.
Building a base of information.
Relationship between bits of information are important.
Curriculum needs to be organized to reveal important relationships.
We all construct meaning, therefore we often learn different things.
All need an awareness of ourselves as thinkers/learners.
All need to develop strategies/skills in learning to learn.
Use videos, class demonstrations, readings, case studies, debates.

Like behaviourism, cognitive learning approaches are still teacher led, but learning is far more active for the learners. They are more involved in lessons and are given tasks, for example, problem solving. They are based on the idea that there are thought processes behind behaviour and that changes in behaviour are observed as an indicator of what is going on in the learners head. Learners should be encouraged to discover the underlying nature of a topic or problem (in other words, the relationship), with instruction based on the laws of organization. Petty (1998) suggests that cognitivist theorists believe that education is more than simply communicating facts and procedures to memory; its main benefit is the development of thinking skills. As Skinner (1964, p. 21) put it, 'Education is what survives when what has been learned has been forgotten.'

Humanistic theory

Facilitation of learning (is the key to effective learning). The third approach to learning is at the other extreme from Skinner's beliefs. Both behaviourist and cognitive take a scientific approach to learning in terms of the methods they use and the theories they generate. By contrast, the humanistic approach is anti-scientific in the way in which it investigates human beings. The underpinning belief is that we are all unique individuals.

Humanism proposes that we are the product of our own particular circumstances. To understand the individual, we must understand individuals' subjective experience of what it is like to be them (Atkinson et al., 1993).

Humanist learning theory was developed in America in the 1960s and mostly associated with two psychologists, Carl Rogers (client-centred therapy) and Abraham Maslow (hierarchy of needs).

Humanists consider humans to be pro-active unique individuals who exercise free will over their behaviour. For example, Stapleton (2001, p. 21) states, 'We are who we are because that is what we have chosen for ourselves, and no-one else can fully know us simply because of the fact they are not us.'

The term humanistic refers to the variety in the approach to the study of human behaviour. The holistic view of behaviour stresses the importance of studying the entire person. Humanistic theories of learning tend to be highly value driven. They emphasize the natural desire to learn with learners needing to be empowered and have control; therefore the teacher becomes a facilitator.

Carl Rogers (1902–1987) is principally known as the founder of person-centred psychotherapy and almost the inventor of counselling, and he is also a leading figure in the development of humanistic approaches to education.

Humanistic theories of learning tend to be highly value driven and describe what should happen rather than what does happen. It emphasizes the natural desire of everyone to learn. Learners need to be empowered and have control over the learning process, such as self-directed learning. The teacher needs to take a step back and rather than leading the learning become a facilitator of the processes.

Rogers distinguished two types of learning: cognitive (academic knowledge such as psychology or multiplication tables) and experiential (applied knowledge such as learning about engines in order to repair a car). The key to the distinction is that experiential learning addresses the needs and wants of the learner and is equivalent to personal change and growth. Rogers felt that all human beings have a natural desire to learn; the role of the teacher is to facilitate such learning. This includes (1) setting a positive climate for learning, (2) clarifying the purposes of the learner(s), (3) organizing and making available learning resources, (4) balancing intellectual and emotional components of learning and (5) sharing feelings and thoughts with learners but not dominating. Learning is facilitated when (1) the student participates completely in the learning process and has control over its nature and direction; (2) it is primarily based upon direct confrontation with practical, social, personal or research problems; and (3) self-evaluation is the principal method of assessing progress or success. Rogers also emphasizes the importance of learning to learn and an openness to change. Roger's theory of learning originates from his views about psychotherapy and humanistic approach to psychology. It applies primarily to adult learners and has influenced other theories of adult learning: (1) Significant learning takes place when the subject matter is relevant to the personal interests of the student, (2) learning which is threatening to the self (e.g., new attitudes or perspectives) are more easily assimilated when external threats are at a minimum, (3) learning proceeds faster when the threat to the self is low and (4) self-initiated learning is the most lasting and pervasive.

Considerations of other leading humanist theorists include Malcolm Knowles and Abraham Maslow. Malcolm Knowles' attempts to develop a distinctive conceptual basis for adult education and learning via the notion of andragogy became very widely discussed and used in the second half of the twentieth century. He also wrote popular works on self-direction and on group work. His work was a significant factor in reorienting adult educators from 'educating people' to 'helping them learn'. Andragogy consists of learning strategies focused on adults. It is often interpreted as the process of engaging adult learners with the structure of learning experience. Knowles theory has seven main assumptions linked to motivation.

Adults should acquire a mature understanding of themselves. They should understand their needs, motivations, interests, capacities and goals. They should be able to look at themselves objectively and maturely. They should accept themselves and respect themselves for what they are, while striving earnestly to become better.

Adults should develop an attitude of acceptance, love, and respect towards others. This is the attitude on which all human relations depend. Adults must learn to distinguish between people and ideas, and to challenge ideas without threatening people. Ideally, this attitude will go beyond acceptance, love, and respect, to empathy and the sincere desire to help others.

Adults should develop a dynamic attitude towards life. They should accept the fact of change and should think of themselves as always changing. They should acquire the habit of looking at every experience as an opportunity to learn and should become skilful in learning from it.

Adults should learn to react to the causes, not the symptoms, of behaviour. Solutions to problems lie in their causes, not in their symptoms. We have learned to apply this lesson in the physical world but have yet to learn to apply it in human relations.

Adults should acquire the skills necessary to achieve the potentials of their personalities. Every person has capacities that, if realized, will contribute to the well-being of himself and of society. To achieve these potentials requires skills of many kinds—vocational, social, recreational, civic, artistic and the like. It should be a goal of education to give each individual those skills necessary for him to make full use of his capacities.

Adults should understand the essential values in the capital of human experience. They should be familiar with the heritage of knowledge, the great ideas, the great traditions, of the world in which they live. They should understand and respect the values that bind men together.

Adults should understand their society and should be skilful in directing social change. In a democracy, the people participate in making decisions that affect the entire social order. It is imperative, therefore, that every factory worker, every salesman, every politician, every housewife know enough about government, economics, international affairs and other aspects of the social order to be able to take part in them intelligently (taken from Knowles, 1950).

We can use andragogy as the essential application of humanistic principles at the beginning of any learning activity. At the beginning of the session a tutor should

establish a climate of equality and mutual respect,
determine the expectations of the learners,
involve them in planning the objectives and lessons,
acknowledge the value of their experiences.

This kind of opening takes a humanistic approach and can lead to the main body of the session using the most appropriate approach to what is to be learned and how much the learners already know. The key to successful adult learning is to gain agreement upfront.

Abraham Maslow's hierarchy of needs is represented in the shape of a pyramid, with the largest and lowest levels of needs at the bottom and the need for self-actualization at the top (Figure 3.3).

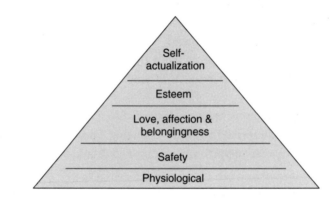

Figure 3.3 Maslow's hierarchy of needs

Applied to the classroom, each part of the pyramid could be associated with the following:

- Physiological

    Reduced price and free lunch programmes
    Correct room temperatures
    Sufficient toilet breaks
    Refreshment breaks

- Safety

    Well-planned lessons carried out in an orderly fashion
    Controlled classroom behaviours

Emergency procedures well planned, discussed and practiced

Fair discipline

Consistent expectations

Attitude of teacher: accepting and non-judgemental, pleasant, nonthreatening

Provide praise for correct responses instead of punishment for incorrect responses

- Love and belonging

    1. With regard to teacher–student relationships

    Teacher personality: empathetic, considerate and interested in the individual; patient; fair; able to self-disclose; positive attitude; good listener

    Use one-on-one instruction

    Provide positive comments and feedback rather than negative

    Get to know students (likes, dislikes, concerns)

    Be available for students by being pastoral and personal as well as academic tutorial support

    Listen to students

    Be supportive

    Have appropriate learning support assistants

    Show that you value students thoughts, opinions and judgements

    Show trust of students by providing opportunities for responsibility

    2. With regard to student–student relationships

    Class meetings

    Class discussions

    Peer tutoring

    Provide situations requiring mutual trust

    Show and tell, sharing achievements

- Esteem

    1. Self-esteem

    Develop new knowledge based on background knowledge so as to help ensure success (scaffolding)

    Pace instruction to fit individual need

    Focus on strengths and assets

    Take individual needs and abilities into account when planning lessons and carrying them out

    Teach and model learning strategies

    Base new teaching, strategies and plans on learning outcomes

    Be alert to student difficulties and intervene as soon as possible

    Be available and approachable so students having difficulties feel comfortable coming for help

    Involve all students in class participation and responsibilities

    When necessary to discipline, do as privately as possible

2. Respect from others

> Develop a classroom environment where students are positive and non-judgemental
> Award programmes for jobs well done
> Providing deserved positions of status
> Develop and carry out a curriculum to encourage children to be empathetic and good listeners
> Employ cooperative learning in such a way as to develop trust between group members
> Involve students in activities of importance and worthiness

- Knowledge and understanding

> Allow students time to explore areas of curiosity
> Provide lessons that are intellectually challenging
> Plan lessons that connect areas of learning and have students compare and contrast to search for relationships
> Use a discovery approach to learning whenever possible
> Have students approach topics of learning from various angles
> Provide opportunities for philosophical thought and discussion
> Get students involved in intellectually challenging programmes

- Aesthetic

> Organize classroom materials in a neat and appealing way
> Display student work in an appealing manner
> Put up interesting and colourful wall hangings
> Replace overly worn classroom materials periodically
> Create varied appealing and interesting learning areas
> Rooms painted in pleasing colours
> Large window areas
> Well-maintained physical surroundings (keeping walls painted, desks clean and repaired)
> Clean rooms
> Fresh-smelling rooms

- Self-actualization

> Expect students to do their best
> Give students freedom to explore and discover on their own
> Make learning meaningful – connect to 'real' life
> Plan lessons involving metacognitive activities
> Get students involved in self-expressive projects
> Allow students to be involved in creative activities and projects

Humanists consider humans to be pro-active unique individuals who exercise free will over their behaviour. Humanist techniques engage the learner in an intense, personal way. They draw upon the wisdom and experience of the participants. They are based on proven successes in counselling, therapy and personal growth, while the behaviourist techniques manipulate people into learning things that they do not care about and do not consider real human behaviour. Humanism draws on people's experiences, treats people as adults, adapts to the diverse needs and expectations of the learners, develops critical thinking and promotes initiative and self-directed learning.

Linking the learning theories to domains of learning and classroom practices

Table 3.1 shows which teaching and learning strategy fits into each learning theory and would best cover the learning outcome.

Table 3.1 Learning domains and learning theories

Domain of learning	Humanist	Cognitivist	Behaviourist
Cognitive	Inductive discussion	Lecture/film	Multiple choice
Knowledge	Inductive game	Graphic illustration	Memorization
Transmit information	Debrief experience	Panel/interview	Association
Verify information	Relevance discussion	Class presentation	Question with answer
	Active elaboration	Reading	
	Confirmatory discussion	Question and answer	
		Review	
		Test	
Psychomotor	Discuss action	Lists steps	Behavioural model
Skill	Visualize action	Demonstration	Behavioural samples
Induce response	Inductive case study	Success stories	Prompting
Strengthen response (practice)	Mental rehearsal project	Case study	Worksheets
Apply the skill	Action plan	Coaching/feedback	Skill drill (game)
	Planning guide		Simulation
	Elaboration		Role play
	Contract		Realistic practice
			Job aid prompts
			On-job performance
Affective	Self-assessment	Authority statement	Assessment
Attitude	Encounter experience	Vicarious experience	Pleasant experience
	Discussion of beliefs	Debate	Reinforcement
	Reverse role play	Testimony	
	Guided reflection		
	Group decision		

Table 3.1 provides a guide to selecting learning activities. It shows how the typical techniques of each approach align with the classical domains of learning for writing learning outcomes. The cognitivist category lists the most tools for communicating knowledge; the behaviourist category lists the least. The reverse is true when it comes to inducing and strengthening skill responses. Any of the three approaches is viable, but the impact on peak performance will be greater if the strengths and weaknesses of each are taken into account.

Learning theories review

- Behaviourist:

  Premise: Learning occurs primarily through the reinforcement of desired responses.
  Concept of learning: Learning is a relatively permanent change in behaviour.
  Key terms: behaviour, conditioning, reinforcement, learning hierarchies.

- Cognitive:

  Premise: Learning occurs primarily through exposure to logically presented information.
  Concept of learning: Learning is a process of constructing new meaning.
  Key terms: cognition, discovery learning, insightful learning, meaningful learning.

- Humanist:

  Premise: Learning occurs primarily through reflection on personal experience.
  Concept of learning: Learning is a process of self-development.
  Key terms: self-actualization, individual needs, intrinsic motivation.

Surface and deep learning

Studies have shown that the student's conception of what learning is can predict the quality of their learning. There is an enormous research base verifying this idea and its importance.

The Jabberwocky exercise

Read the passage below and answer the following questions:

Twas brillig, and the slithy toves
Did gyre and gimble in the wabe
All mimsy were the borogoves
And the mome raths outgrabe
Question 1: What were the slithy toves doing in the wabe?
Question 2: How would you describe the state of the borogoves?
Question 3: What can you say about the mome raths?
Question 4: Why were the borogroves mimsy?
Question 5: How effective was the mome raths' strategy?

Most people get the following answers:

1: Gyring and gambling
2: They are all mimsy
3. They outgrabe

Questions 4, and 5 are impossible to answer as we do not have enough information to understand what is being asked by these questions. That is, we cannot find meaning for it out of pure speculation. The purpose of this activity was to show you that for lower learning (surface learning) we do not require learners to make sense of material. However, tasks which require deeper learning require students to make meanings or 'constructs'. Learning without understanding is called rote learning or surface learning. The learner does not need to make sense of the material to get the right answer.

There are five levels of surface to deep learning; Level 1-3 are 'surface' and Levels 4-5 are deep.

1. Learning is an increase in knowledge.
2. Learning is memorizing.
3. Learning is acquiring facts or procedures which are to be used.
4. Learning is making sense. Students make active attempts to abstract meaning.
5. Learning is understanding reality: 'When you have really learnt something you kind of see things you couldn't see before. Everything changes' (Marton and Saljo, 1984)

Surface learning can be described as shallow or superficial as it is simply the recalling of factual information. Learning need to have the ability to memorize and regurgitate information which will probably be lost following a simple test of the memorize information (see STM and LTM). As no links to themes are made between the facts, the learning is passive. However, deeper learning requires organization and structuring information to relate to existing knowledge or understanding. This allows learners to challenge new concepts examining the logical development to determine what is significant.

Taxonomies of learning

Benjamin Bloom (1956) identified three domains of educational activities:

Cognitive: mental skills (*Knowledge*)
Affective: growth in feelings or emotional areas (*Attitude*)
Psychomotor: manual or physical skills (*Skills*) (refer back to Chapter 2 on domains of learning)

Bloom believed that education should focus on 'mastery' of subjects and the promotion of higher forms of thinking, rather than a simple transferring of facts. Bloom demonstrated that most teaching tended to be focused on fact transfer and information recall – the lowest level of training – rather than true meaningful personal development, and this remains a central challenge for educators and trainers.

Blooms taxonomies link directly back to the domains of learning we studied in Chapter 2; however, these are now expanded to show how we can encourage deeper learning using the taxonomies.

- Major categories in the psychomotor domain (listed in increasing difficulty – surface to deep learning):

  1. Imitation – observes skill and tries to repeat it.
  2. Manipulation – performs skill according to instruction rather than observation.
  3. Precision – reproduces a skill with accuracy, proportion and exactness. Usually performed independent of original source.
  4. Articulation – combines one or more skills in sequence with harmony and consistency.
  5. Naturalization – completes one or more skills with ease and becomes automatic.

- Major categories in the cognitive domain (listed in increasing difficulty – surface to deep learning):

  1. Knowledge – recognition and recall of information.
  2. Comprehension – interprets, translates or summarizes given information.
  3. Application – uses information in a situation different from original learning context.
  4. Analysis – separates whole into parts until relationships are clear.
  5. Synthesis – combines elements to form new entity from original one.
  6. Evaluation – involves acts of decision making or judging based on criteria or rationale.

- Major categories in the affective domain (listed in increasing difficulty – surface to deep learning):

  1. Receiving – aware of passively attending certain stimuli, for example, listening.
  2. Responding – complies to given expectations be creating stimuli.
  3. Valuing – displays behaviour consistent with single belief or attitude in situations where not forced to obey.
  4. Organizing – committed to set values as displayed by behaviour.
  5. Characterizing – total behaviour consistent with internalized values.

At its basic level, the Taxonomy provides a simple, quick and easy checklist to develop your learning outcomes. You can develop learning by varying the questions that are asked to the learners. This means that simple questions such as 'what do you think this means?' can be developed into more complex questions such as 'how can this be analysed?'

The more detailed elements within each domain provide additional reference points for learning design and evaluation – whether for a single lesson, session or activity; or training need; or for an entire course, programme or syllabus – across a large group of trainees or students.

At its most complex, Bloom's Taxonomy is continuously evolving, through the work of academics following in the footsteps of Bloom's early associates, as a fundamental concept for the development of formalized education across the world. Recently in a Scottish CPD event for teachers, the then Education Minister Peter Peacock spoke of the need to ensure that the Curriculum for Excellence is taught by 'teachers for excellence'. Mr. Peacock said, "*Teachers must develop enhanced expertise in teaching practices, learning new skills and increasing knowledge. All teachers must analyse their practice and reflect on how they help young people cultivate knowledge and skill to improve their own work and develop higher order learning using Bloom's taxonomy as an example.*" (www.ltscotland.uk, accessed 8th June 2010)

Using Bloom's work, we can ensure we move learning from a surface approach to a deeper understanding and application. A deep approach produces longer lasting learning, and deep learners do better in examinations than surface learners. Deep learners structure their understanding; surface learners tend to just remember unstructured detail. Deep learners look for, and find, links with previous learning, surface learners do not. Surface learning produces marginally higher scores on tests of factual recall immediately after studying. However, surface learners forget this quickly, and as little as a week later deep learners score higher even in tests of factual recall. Coursework grades are a better predictor of long-term recall than exam grades.

Most students, however, can adopt both a surface and a deep approach to their learning. Students have been found to make their choice depending on the assessment and the teacher's requirements. A small proportion of students seem only to adopt a surface approach. Some programmes of study have developed learners' deep learning skills when these students have arrived with only surface skills.

Methods to encourage deep learning

1. Create intrinsic motivation – Intrinsic motivation is interest in the subject and the tasks set for their own sake. Foster curiosity, interest, passion, real-world implications of what they are studying, creativity, problem solving and individual responses to the material.
2. Learner activity – Students need to be active rather than passive, and the activity must be planned, reflected upon and processed and also be related to any abstract concepts.
3. Interaction with others – Group work requires negotiating meaning, expressing and manipulating ideas. Discussion promotes high quality learning.
4. Well-structured knowledge base – Without existing concepts, it is impossible to make sense of new concepts. It is vital that students' existing knowledge and experience are brought out in the learning. The structure of the topic must be made clear.

Practical strategies to encourage a deep approach (Marton and Saljo, 1976)

- Teaching by asking (instead of teaching by telling) – use assertive questioning, sometimes called guided discovery.

  1. Write up a question.
  2. Split students into groups to work on the questions.
  3. Get feedback from the groups.
  4. Write up good ideas.
  5. 'Top up' their understanding.
  6. Summarize what they should have learned.

- Use a problem-centred approach – rather than teaching the content, give students a problem and require them to study the content in order to solve the problem.
- Use a case-study approach – give a case study or scenario with questions or other tasks to give the topic vocational relevance and require students to think 'holistically'.

- Set tasks which require a creative response – design a leaflet, poster, presentation device etc. Give constructive suggestions for improvement in a given situation. Solve a problem; write an essay, report or criticism. Design a policy or strategy. Design and carry out a survey with a questionnaire.
- Ask higher order questions from Bloom's taxonomy, not just 'jabberwocky' or low-order questions – require students to be involved in analysis, synthesis and evaluation.
- Structure lessons around questions rather than answers to develop curiosity – 'why do trees lose their leaves in winter?' Or 'how should a business run its meetings?'

Simply stated, deep learning involves the critical analysis of new ideas, linking them to already known concepts and principles, and leads to understanding and long-term retention of concepts so that they can be used for problem solving in unfamiliar contexts. Deep learning promotes understanding and application for life. In contrast, surface learning is the tacit acceptance of information and memorization as isolated and unlinked facts. It leads to superficial retention of material for examinations and does not promote understanding or long-term retention of knowledge and information (Haughton, 2004).

Good classroom communication skills

Teaching is generally considered as only 50 per cent knowledge and 50 per cent interpersonal or communication skills. For a teacher, it is not only important to give a quality lecture but it is also more important for the presentation of a lesson in class. Communication skills for teachers are as important as their in-depth knowledge of the particular subject which they teach.

Teachers should be aware of the importance of communication skills in teaching. They must also realize that all students have different levels of strengths and weaknesses; they can also have significant barriers to learning. It is only through communication skills that a teacher can introduce creative and effective solutions to the problems of the students. Therefore, a teacher can enhance the learning process through the use of effective communication skills.

Why do we need to communicate?

We communicate for a variety of reasons – to change behaviour, for instance, using verbal and nonverbal cues to get the required behavioural response, to get action or persuade using skills which elicit an actioned response. We use communication skills to ensure learners understand what they are supposed to be doing and to give and receive information.

The most common ways to communication is through the spoken word, the written word, visual images and body language.

Communication is the process of sending and receiving information among people; however, sometimes the information does not get to the sender/receiver due to 'distortion'. Some examples of distortion or the barriers to understanding/listening are as follows:

Perceptions	Emotions
Language	Inflections
Personal interests	Environment – noise
Semantics	Preconceived notions/expectations
Wordiness	Attention span
Physical hearing problem	Speed of thought

It is not only what you say in the classroom that is important but it is also how you say it that can make the difference to students. Nonverbal messages are an essential component of communication in the teaching process. Teachers should be aware of nonverbal behaviour in the classroom for three major reasons:

1. An awareness of nonverbal behaviour will allow you to become better receivers of students' messages.
2. You will become a better sender of signals that reinforce learning.
3. This mode of communication increases the degree of the perceived psychological closeness between teacher and student.

Some major areas of nonverbal behaviours to explore are

Eye contact: This is an important channel of interpersonal communication, helps regulate the flow of communication. It signals interest in others. Eye contact with audiences increases the speakers' credibility. Teachers who make eye contact open the flow of communication and convey interest, concern, warmth and credibility.

Facial expressions: Smiling is a powerful cue that transmits happiness, friendliness, warmth, liking and affliction. Therefore, if you smile frequently you will be perceived as more likable, friendly, warm and approachable. Smiling is often contagious and students will react favourably and learn more.

Gestures: If you fail to gesture while speaking, you may be perceived as boring, stiff and unanimated. A lively and animated teaching style captures students' attention, makes the material more interesting, facilitates learning and provides a bit of entertainment. Head nods, a form of gesture, communicates positive reinforcement to students and indicates that you are listening.

Posture and body orientation: You communicate numerous messages by the way you walk, talk, stand and sit. Standing erect, but not rigid, and leaning slightly forward communicates to students that you are approachable, respective and friendly. Furthermore, interpersonal closeness results when you and your students face each other. Speaking with your back turned or looking at the floor or ceiling should be avoided; it communicates disinterest to your class.

Proximity: Cultural norms dictate a comfortable distance for interaction with students. You should look for signals of discomfort caused by invading students' space. Some of these are rocking, leg swinging, tapping and gaze aversion. Typically, in large college classes space invasion is not a problem. In fact, there is usually too much distance. To counteract this, move around the classroom to increase interaction with your students. Increasing proximity enables you to make better eye contact and increase the opportunities for students to speak.

Paralinguistics: This facet of nonverbal communication includes such vocal elements as tone, pitch, rhythm, timbre, loudness and inflection. For maximum teaching effectiveness, learn to vary these six elements of your voice. One of the major criticisms is of instructors who speak in a monotone. Listeners perceive these as boring and dull. Students report that they learn less and lose interest more quickly when listening to teachers who have not learned to moderate their voices.

Humour: This is often overlooked as a teaching tool, and it is too often not encouraged in college classrooms. Laughter releases stress and tension for both instructor and students. You should develop the ability to laugh at yourself and encourage students to do the same. It fosters a friendly classroom environment that facilitates learning.

Obviously, adequate knowledge of the subject matter is crucial to your success; however, it is not the only crucial element. Creating a climate that facilitates learning and retention demands good nonverbal and verbal skills. To improve your nonverbal skills, record your speaking on videotape. Then ask a colleague in communications to suggest refinement. Quite often, watching the videotape back yourself can often lead to some pertinent self-evaluation of your nonverbal skills.

Verbal communication

Verbal communication is one way for people to communicate face to face. Some of the key components of verbal communication are sound, words, speaking and language. Oral communication is a process whereby information is transferred from a sender to receiver usually by a verbal means, but visual aid can support the process (see previous section on sender/receiver and distortion). The receiver could be an individual person, a group of people or even an audience. There are a few different oral communication strategies, such as discussion, speeches, presentations. However, often when you communicate face to face, the body language and your voice tonality has a bigger impact than the actual words that you are saying. According to research by Petty (1998),

> 55 per cent of the impact is determined by the body language, for example, posture, gesture, eye contact,
> 38 per cent by the tone of your voice,
> 7 per cent by the content of your words in a communication process.

Therefore, the *how you say it* has a major impact on the receiver. You have to capture the attention of the audience and connect with them. For example, when two people are saying the same joke, one of them could make the audience die laughing because of his good body language and tone of voice. However, the second person who has the exact same words could make the audience stare at one another in exasperation.

In an oral communication, it is possible to have visual aids helping you to provide more precise information. Often, we use a PowerPoint presentation related to our speech to facilitate or enhance the communication process. This assists with communication techniques by adding in the written word and visual images to enhance the learning.

How can we make verbal communication more effective?

> Clear, good pronunciation of words
> Simple language that is easy to understand
> No jargon, unless it is explained
> No abbreviations or acronyms unless previously explained
> Speak to aid understanding and not to impress

Effective communication skills in education are easily identified by successful learners. Just as any business cannot succeed if the leadership is not effective, neither can students if the educator is not communicating properly. Effective communication in education produces students who understand the information and are motivated to learn more and perform well. When effective communication is the cornerstone, both the students and tutor are satisfied with their roles.

In teacher training courses, educators describe the responsibility of the tutor is to verbally communicate in such a way that every student will understand. Although this is true, it must be considered that each student learns differently and at various rates. Communication must be effective in order for students to succeed, but each student has a different way to process information. This leaves responsibility on the student to effectively listen.

The benefits of effective communication from a teachers' perspective are clear and concise information, obvious direction and authority. When a teacher effectively communicates, they will be able to speak and demonstrate each lesson, clearly avoiding and clarifying confusion in the information. Effective communication also commands direction, which provides the students with a road map of where the students are and where they're going. When a teacher can effectively communicate the knowledge they posses, the students will respond with respect.

Summary of key points

In this chapter, we have looked at learning theories and their application to education and the classroom. Each learning theory has been discussed in detail showing clear advantages and disadvantages for each strategy. Visual images have illustrated this well, showing clear interpretation of the theorists who are associated with each learning theory. It is hoped you will use the knowledge gained from looking at the learning theories to link to your curriculum and lesson planning. The chapter then progresses to identifying Bloom's taxonomies of learning and how this links to surface and deeper learning. Hopefully the key points shown will assist you with writing differentiated learning outcomes that challenge your more able learners. The final section focused on the development of communications skills. We have looked closely at the importance of nonverbal communication as well as verbal, written and visual communication. We have previously argued that teaching is not an impossible profession. It can be argued that teaching, just like learning, is a discipline. This means that it is important to learn from teaching experiences. Reflect on these experiences. Retain what is positive. Amend and adapt what has been less than positive. This is essentially at the centre of the craft of teaching.

This chapter links to the following SVUK professional standards:

Professional values

AS 1: All learners, their progress and development, their learning goals and aspirations and the experience they bring to their learning.

AS 4: Reflection and evaluation of their own practice and their continuing professional development as teachers.

AS 7: Improving the quality of their practice.

BS 1: Maintaining an inclusive, equitable and motivating learning environment.

BS 3: Communicating effectively and appropriately with learners to enhance learning.

CS 4: Developing good practice in teaching own specialist area.

DS 2: Learner participation in the planning of learning.

DS 3: Evaluation of own effectiveness in planning learning.

FS 2: Providing support for learners within the boundaries of the teacher role.

FS 3: Maintaining own professional knowledge in order to provide information on opportunities for progression in own specialist area.

Professional knowledge and understanding

AK 1.1: What motivates learners to learn and the importance of learners' experience and aspirations.

AK 3.1: Issues of equality, diversity and inclusion.

AK 4.1: Principles, frameworks and theories which underpin good practice in learning and teaching.

AK 4.2: The impact of own practice on individuals and their learning.

AK 5.1: Ways to communicate and collaborate with colleagues and/or others to enhance learners' experience.

BK 1.1: Ways to maintain a learning environment in which learners feel safe and supported.

BK 1.2: Ways to develop and manage behaviours which promote respect for and between others and create an equitable and inclusive learning environment.

BK 1.3: Ways of creating a motivating learning environment.

BK 2.1: Principles of learning and ways to provide learning activities to meet curriculum requirements and the needs of all learners.

BK 2.2: Ways to engage, motivate and encourage active participation of learners and learner independence.

⇨

BK 2.3: The relevance of learning approaches, preferences and skills to learner progress.

BK 3.1: Effective and appropriate use of different forms of communication informed by relevant theories and principles.

BK 3.2: A range of listening and questioning techniques to support learning.

BK 3.3: Ways to structure and present information and ideas clearly.

BK 3.4: Barriers and aids to effective communication.

BK 3.5: Systems for communication within own organization.

CK 2.1: Ways to convey enthusiasm for own specialist area to learners.

CK 3.1: Teaching and learning theories and strategies relevant to own specialist area.

CK 3.2: Ways to identify individual learning needs and potential barriers to learning in own specialist area.

DK 1.1: How to plan appropriate, effective, coherent and inclusive learning programmes that promote equality and engage with diversity.

DK 2.1: The importance of including learners in the planning process.

DK 2.2: Ways to negotiate appropriate individual goals with learners.

Professional practice

AP 4.1: Use relevant theories of learning to support the development of practice in learning and teaching.

AP 4.2: Reflect on and demonstrate commitment to improvement of own personal and teaching skills through regular evaluation and use of feedback.

AP 4.3: Share good practice with others and engage in continuing professional development through reflection, evaluation and appropriate use of research.

AP 6.2: Demonstrate good practice through maintaining a learning environment which conforms to statutory requirements and promotes equality, including appropriate consideration of the needs of children, young people and vulnerable adults.

AP 7.3: Use feedback to develop own practice within the organization's systems.

BP 1.1: Establish a purposeful learning environment where learners feel safe, secure, confident and valued.

BP 1.3: Create a motivating environment which encourages learners to reflect on, evaluate and make decisions about their learning.

BP 2.1: Provide learning activities which meet curriculum requirements and the needs of all learners.

BP 2.4: Apply flexible and varied delivery methods as appropriate to teaching and learning practice.

BP 2.5: Encourage learners to use their own life experiences as a foundation for their development.

BP 2.6: Evaluate the efficiency and effectiveness of own teaching, including consideration of learner feedback and learning theories.

BP 3.1: Communicate effectively and appropriately using different forms of language and media, including written, oral and nonverbal communication, and new and emerging technologies to enhance learning.

BP 3.2: Use listening and questioning techniques appropriately and effectively in a range of learning contexts.

BP 3.3: Structure and present information clearly and effectively.

BP 3.4: Evaluate and improve own communication skills to maximize effective communication and overcome identifiable barriers to communication.

BP 3.5: Identify and use appropriate organizational systems for communicating with learners and colleagues.

⇨

CP 2.1: Implement appropriate and innovative ways to enthuse and motivate learners about own specialist area.

CP 3.1: Apply appropriate strategies and theories of teaching and learning to own specialist area.

CP 3.2: Work with learners to address particular individual learning needs and overcome identified barriers to learning.

DP 1.2: Plan teaching sessions which meet the aims and needs of individual learners and groups, using a variety of resources, including new and emerging technologies.

Self-assessment questions

Learning theories

1. Learning is a relatively permanent change in . . . .
2. How does advertising work?
3. Who has used operant conditioning on you, and what did they get you to do?
4. Behaviourists believe that all behaviour is . . . .
5. Name a major cognitivist theorist.
6. Name a Humanist theorist who has been discussed within this chapter.
7. What is surface learning?
8. State three ways to apply deeper learning strategies in the classroom.

Moving on feature

This chapter has introduced learning theories which feature in every aspect of your planning and presentation of session. These theories also impact upon how you manage your classroom (see Chapter 4). The chapter also focuses on the use of surface and deeper learning which you should consider when writing learning outcomes and planning activities for learners. The next chapter on classroom management uses learning theories to help you decide on appropriate teaching and learning strategies which will engage, interest and motivate learners and how you can use these strategies for classroom praise and rewards. Continue to think about positive communication skills when studying classroom management as you need to develop your own skills and those of your learners.

Further Reading

Maslow, A. (1987), *Motivation and Personality* (3rd edition). New York: Harper and Row.

Petty, G. (1998), *Teaching Today* (2nd edition). Cheltenham. Nelson Thornes.

Rogers, C. (1983), *Freedom to Learn.* New York. Merrill.

Training and Development Journal (December, 1990), Behaviourism Versus Cognitivism.

An excellent textbook that is written in an accessible way and makes clear links to applying theory to practice.

Tummons, J. (2007), *Becoming a Professional Tutor in the Lifelong Learning Sector*. Exeter: Learning Matters.

A valuable textbook which the author uses to deliver the Theories and Principle module for Teesside University Professional Graduate Certificate in Education.

References

Atherton, J. S. (2009), *Learning and Teaching; Cognitive Theories of Learning*. Available: http://www.learningandteaching.info/learning/cognitive.htm Accessed: 27 January 2010.

Atkinson, R. L., Atkinson R. C., Smith E. E. and Bem D. J. (1993), *Introduction to Psychology* (11th edition). Fort Worth, TX: Harcourt Brace Jovanovich.

Bloom, B. S. (ed.), (1956), *Taxonomy of Educational Objectives, The Classification of Educational Goals – Handbook I: Cognitive Domain*. New York: McKay.

Haughton, E. (2004), *Learning and Teaching Theory*. Available: http://www.learning-theories.com Accessed: 27 January 2010.

Huitt, W. & Hummel, J. (1999), *Behaviourist Learning Theory*. Available: http://www.edpsycinteractive.org/edpsyppt/Theory/behthr.ppt Accessed: 16 March 2010.

Knowles, M. S. (1950), *Informal Adult Education*. Chicago: Association Press.

Marton, F. and Saljo, R. (1976), 'On Qualitative Differences in Learning – 2: Outcome as a function of the learner's conception of the task'. *British Journal of Educational Psychology, 46*: 115-27.

Petty, G. (1998), *Teaching Today* (2nd edition). Cheltenham: Nelson Thornes.

Skinner, B. F. (1964), *Science and Human Behaviour*. New York: Macmillan.

Stapleton, M (2001), *Psychology in Practice*. London: Hodder & Stoughton.

Tulving, E. (1985), 'How Many Memory Systems Are There?'. *American Psychologist, 40*: 385-98.

4 Classroom Management

Learning Outcomes

After reading this chapter you should be able to

> identify and analyse some of the ways that psychology can be used to enhance classroom management,
>
> critically appraise some of the ways that psychology can be applied to classroom management.

Introduction

This chapter considers the discipline of psychology and discusses how psychology can be applied to classroom management in order to improve professional practice. It can be argued that each school of psychology has a different understanding of what constitutes the self. This understanding is outlined, analysed and critically appraised in order to explore how psychology can be applied to classroom management. Throughout the chapter, there are formative activities that reinforce learning in relation to the main psychological paradigms (or models) that are of relevance for the Lifelong Learning Sector. The chapter explores how the psychological perspectives of behaviourism, humanism, biological, psychodynamic and cognitive theory can be applied to classroom management. The chapter concludes by assessing the merits of each of the perspectives in respect of the contribution being made to classroom management.

Defining the discipline of psychology

Activity 4.1

What is your understanding of the word psychology?

Feedback

Psychology is an academic discipline that studies a vast range of human and animal behaviour. Psychologists are not mind readers, and they do not necessarily have access to our thoughts. They do not work solely with people who are 'mentally ill' or people who are 'emotionally disturbed'. These are common delusions and misinterpretations of the discipline.

'Psychology' is not as easy to define as it might initially appear. It is more than just a word. To a lay person an immediate reaction may be to associate psychology with 'reading peoples' minds' or 'analysing aspects of human behaviour'. A dictionary definition of psychology may give a precise explanation, but this precision can disguise the complexity of the subject. An example dictionary definition is that psychology can be understood as being *the scientific study of all forms of human and animal behaviour* (online dictionary).

Psychology is relevant for the Lifelong Learning Sector because it gives explanations for 'challenging behaviour'. This means that having some awareness of psychology can increase your awareness of classroom management.

Origins of psychology

The word psychology is derived from the Greek words 'psyche', meaning 'mind' and 'logos', meaning 'study', so a literal translation of the word is 'the study of the mind'. Malim and Birch (1998: 3) claim that the discipline began in 1879 when Wilhelm Wundt opened the first psychology laboratory at the University of Leipzig in Germany. Wundt focused upon 'introspection' or observing and analysing the structure of conscious mental processes. It was the emphasis placed upon measurement and control of thinking processes that marked the separation of psychology from its parent discipline philosophy.

The rise of behaviourism

Malim and Birch (1998: 8) argue that by 1920 the usefulness of 'introspection' was questioned. John B. Watson was one of a number of academics who believed that it was wrong to focus upon introspection because this approach to studying psychology is immeasurable, and it invalidates the discipline's scientific credentials. Consequently, Watson dedicated himself to the study of what has become known as 'behaviourism' or human behaviour that is measurable and observable. Behaviourism remained the dominant force in psychology over the next 30 years, especially in the United States. The emphasis was placed upon identifying the external factors that produce changes in behaviour, learning or conditioning using a 'stimuli response' model.

Competing perspectives

As with many philosophical and sociological perspectives, psychology is characterized by competing paradigms or models of thought, with theorists becoming grouped together according to which perspective they adopt. Malim and Birch (1998: 9) argue that an interesting reaction to behaviourism came in the form of the Gestalt school of psychology that emerged in Austria and Germany in the 1920s popularized by psychologists such as Wolfgang Kohler (1927). This branch of psychology applies the holistic approach of considering that the whole person is greater and more complex than his or her individual characteristics. This in turn complicates a focus upon the external factors producing thoughts and behaviour.

Psychodynamic psychology

A further criticism of behaviourism developed through the twentieth century as a result of the legacy of Sigmund Freud, possibly the most famous psychologist of all. Malim and Birch (1998: 9) argue that Freud proposes that the mind is a combination of conscious and unconscious thoughts. If we accept that this is the case, Freud's theory can be used to challenge behaviourism because it implies that human thought and behaviour is more complex than the behaviourist notion that external variables cause thought and behaviour.

Cognitive psychology

Alongside psychodynamic theory, there emerged a further significant theory that places the emphasis upon thinking processes or cognition, in other words, the ways in which we attain, retain and regain information. Within cognitive psychology, an emphasis is placed on identifying what happens within the mind after a stimulus has been received. The mind is seen as being like an information processor, almost akin to a computer. Malim and Birch (1998: 25) explain this perspective by arguing that *human beings are seen as information processors who absorb information from the outside world, code and interpret it, store and retrieve it.* In a literal revolution of thought, thinking has come back full circle, and the initial criticism of introspection being unlikely to explain the complexity of human thought is asserted within this psychological theory.

Biological psychology

This view is reinforced by some of the current developments within psychology. The scientific advances of the 1990s and beyond in relation to identifying the genetic and hormonal composition of the human mind have generated enormous interest in the idea that thoughts and behaviour are determined by our biology. This may be considered to be a reductionist argument because it reduces complex thoughts and behaviour to a few variables such as hormones and genes. The ideas within biological psychology may prove to be yet another passing paradigm contributing to the ongoing dialogue about the discipline of psychology that in turn will be criticised and revised.

From this initial discussion about what is meant by the word psychology, we can ask a further question in relation to the nature of the human mind. *Is the human mind the same as the human brain?*

Activity 4.2

Do you think that the mind is the same as the brain? List your reasons to support or disagree with this view.

Feedback

One answer to this question is that there is no definite answer. Philosophers have speculated for hundreds, perhaps thousands, of years about what has come to be known as 'the mind–brain problem'. Whether you focus upon the mind or the brain depends upon your fundamental understanding of how psychology should be studied. Many psychological perspectives, such as behaviourism, humanism, psychodynamic and cognitive theories, emphasize the importance of the mind. This is because each of these perspectives has a clear understanding or model of the mind. In contrast, biological perspectives are more likely to place an emphasis upon the genes and hormones influencing the brain.

We can now look at exploring some of the psychological perspectives. This is a way of adding detail to our introductory explanations of what the subject area of psychology is. It is also a means of setting the scene before we look at how psychology can be applied to classroom management within the Lifelong Learning Sector.

The schools of psychology

In Table 4.1, there is a summary of five major schools of psychology together with a brief description of their key features.

These schools of thought are especially useful for the Lifelong Learning Sector because of the influence they have had in shaping the academic concerns of psychology which underpin your work with students. If you are teaching within the Lifelong Learning Sector, you will need to be aware of 'modelling' and 'discussion' as you are working with your students. Knowledge and understanding of the competing perspectives in psychology will help you as a teacher, as these ideas have contributed to the development of educational philosophies. The origins of the psychological schools of thought go back to some of the earliest philosophical ideas to have influenced western thought. The proposition that there are forces beyond the individual that shape social reality goes back to the ideas of the Greek philosopher Plato. This idea is central to behaviourism, so the perspective has its intellectual origins in this classical thought. The notion that individuals interpret their social world as opposed to being ultimately shaped by this world goes back to the ideas of Aristotle (Audi, 1995). This philosophy is of central importance to humanism. In other words, the genesis of the perspective's dominant idea can be traced back to these early times. A summary of each of the key perspectives developing the definitions given in Table 4.1 follows. A definition of each of the key perspectives is given, key figures influencing the perspective are identified and central

Table 4.1 Schools of psychology

School	Key features
Behaviourism	Human behaviour is seen as being shaped by environmental forces and is a collection of learned responses to external stimuli. The key learning process is known as 'conditioning'
Humanism	The individual is seen as being unique, rational and self-determining. Present experience is held to be as important as past experience
Psychodynamic theory	The mind is seen as being a combination of conscious thoughts and the workings of the unconscious mind. The unconscious mind expresses itself through dreams and behaviour we are not consciously aware of
Cognitive theory	This perspective looks at what happens after a stimulus but before a response. The human mind is likened to a computer. People are seen as information processors, selecting, coding, storing and retrieving information when needed
Neurobiological theory	Behaviour is considered as being determined by genetic, physiological and neurobiological factors and processes

terms within each perspective are explained. There is also consideration of how the ideas may be applied to classroom management.

Behaviourism

Behaviourists emphasize the importance of external factors in producing thoughts within the human mind. A key behaviourist idea is that every individual enters the world as a 'clean slate'. The surrounding environment is considered to be the 'chalk' etching its marks upon the 'slate' of the mind. This means that the individual enters the world without a fixed identity and that social factors are responsible for making the individual whosoever he/she becomes. The Jesuit notion of 'giving me the boy and I'll show you the man' equates to this idea. This suggests that we become who we are as a result of factors beyond and outside individuals.

A number of psychologists have become famous members of the behaviourist school of thought. Burrhus Skinner, Edward Thorndike, John Watson and Ivan Pavlov have become synonymous with behaviourist psychology. All of these psychologists share in common the belief that external factors are of critical importance in producing thoughts and behaviour.

The terms 'classical conditioning' and 'operant conditioning' are particularly important within behaviourism. Classical conditioning is associated with the work of Ivan Pavlov. It has become associated with the ways whereby biological responses are regulated by external factors. This produces what has become phrased as a 'conditioned response' where a form of behaviour occurs in association with a particular stimulus. Operant conditioning is a term that has become associated with the work of Burrhus Skinner. It refers to the link that exists between positively affirming behaviour that reinforces a particular stimulus. To give a simple example, if a student responds favourably to a lecturer, the learner is usually praised. This reinforcement of learning through praise is therefore a type of operant conditioning. In the following case study, there is the exemplification of when students may experience classical and operant conditioning.

Case Study

Carrie is 17 years old and she has just started College. She has been in the College for one month, and she has already learned many of the College 'ground rules'. She has noticed that her tutors expect students to attend teaching sessions on time and that mobile phones are expected to be switched off during teaching sessions. At first, a number of the students were confused by the College environment. The sight of all the other 'new faces' made some of the students afraid and anxious because they were unfamiliar with this new learning environment. This association of 'being new to College' and 'anxiety' appears to have helped the students to form friendship groups. Today before lectures started many of the students got into their friendship groups so that they would not stand out and feel anxious. On Friday, Carrie received some feedback on her first piece of College work, her completed Independent Learning Plan (ILP). She felt very pleased at getting positive feedback on her work so early into the programme. Carrie remembered her parents' advice that she should always try her hardest.

The behaviourist emphasis on the importance of the external environment is of interest in considering classroom management. It can be argued that an enabling learning environment is necessary if individual learners are to fulfil their potential. This means that the learning environment needs to be supportive at physical, intellectual, emotional and social levels. The teaching environment ought to stimulate learning through promoting positive emotions. If the classroom is too cold, too warm, too light, too dark, too small or too big, these 'external' factors hold the potential to influence one's ability to 'manage' the classroom.

Humanism

Humanism does acknowledge the importance of environmental factors on the mind, but it places an emphasis upon the individual interpretation of external factors. This means that as opposed to emphasizing the importance of external variables, attention is given to the importance of individuals interpreting social reality. Humanism can be associated with the philosophy of Immanuel Kant and his 'Copernican revolution' of thought (Audi, 1995: 400). As opposed to asking about the reality of the universe, Kant changes the focus of the argument to ask about how individuals understand social reality. Humanism asks a similar question. As opposed to focusing upon how external variables produce thoughts, the humanist emphasis is on how individuals make sense of external variables.

Humanism has become associated with the work of Carl Rogers and Abraham Maslow. Maslow proposes that all humans have a 'hierarchy of needs'. This means that thoughts are influenced by the extent to which these physiological and intellectual needs are being met. Carl Rogers has had a particularly important influence on humanism, and it may be claimed that Rogers is the founding father of psychological humanism. His work is also influential in what is considered as being effective inclusive practice. One of the most important Rogerian ideas to have influenced social care is the proposal that anxiety is a product of what has become termed as a 'would/should dilemma'. This means that an individual wants to do something but they are unable to achieve this wish. According to Rogers, this then generates tension within the individual that in turn produces anxiety.

In applying therapy to resolve the would/should dilemma, Rogers recommends that the therapist must have a 'congruent' or 'genuine' interest in the person. This means that empathy is a central concept to the Rogerian model of client-centred therapy. The ideal aim is to lead the person being counselled to their 'inner beautiful self' so that the individual's would/should dilemma can be overcome.

Rogerian philosophy can be applied to classroom management through considering what is likely to make learners 'anxious'. We have previously emphasized the importance of having a 'positive' or 'accommodating' learning environment. It can be argued that this is more likely to make the learners receptive to the learning process. Rogers would also consider that it is especially important to make sure that communication is as good as possible so that learners know what is required from them during the learning process. This means that 'mixed messages' should not adversely influence the communication process.

A 'congruent' learning process is recommended as learners and teachers develop an environment of mutual respect. Establishing 'ground rules', ensuring that the learning process is characterized by clear boundaries alongside assertive interpersonal relationships, become especially important within this process of humanistic classroom management. It can be argued that this 'ideal' is not always the 'reality' of learning and teaching, and this point is developed later in the chapter.

Activity 4.3

Think about your own personal development. To what extent do you think that your personality has been formed as a result of external environmental factors? To what extent do you think that your personality is a product of your unique personality?

Feedback

Most people would probably accept that their personality is a combination of external environmental variables alongside their own unique personal traits. In other words, the person is a product of factors that are both outside and inside the individual. It is interesting, however, to consider why and when the emphasis placed upon the individual and the environment varies. In this country, particular social, economic and religious variables have influenced the extent to which one's surroundings or one's personality are held accountable for personality development. In the United Kingdom, there are many communities that emphasize self-responsibility. If one claims that the environment is responsible for personal development, this may be regarded as an attempt to disown one's accountability for individual life circumstances. Some of the popular movements of the 1960s and 1970s may have changed this perception, but the prevailing thought in the United Kingdom today would seem to be that individual characteristics are especially important in determining one's personality. This may lessen the importance of the behaviourist perspective and make humanism a more influential explanation of individual circumstances.

Psychodynamic theory

Psychodynamic psychology is associated with the ideas of one of the most famous psychologists, Sigmund Freud. Freud's theory postulates that thoughts are a product of the working of both the conscious and the unconscious mind (Gross, 2001). We have conscious thoughts that we are aware of and unconscious thoughts that appear in our mind in the form of dreams. Moreover, what happens in our conscious mind in turn influences what thoughts filter through to our unconscious mind.

Freud considers that there are three especially important components to every individual (Gross, 1999: 591). There is the 'id' or biological physiology of maleness and femaleness. There is the 'ego' or social self to regulate our biological 'id'. There is also the 'superego' existing beyond the individual that generates a common understanding of our social identity.

Freud claims that all individuals go through a number of stages of development. From zero to one, a child is considered to be in an oral stage of development. This means that the infant is preoccupied with its mouth. This then leads to the anal stage of development from one to two, when the infant becomes aware of its capacity to excrete and urinate. The next developmental stage is the phallic stage of development when boys and girls become increasingly aware of biological maleness and femaleness. Freud claims that this occurs between the ages of three to six resulting in a close relationship between a boy and his mother and a girl and her father. After the phallic stage of development, there is what Freud terms as a latent phase of development. This occurs between the ages of 6 and 12 as the individual becomes more concerned with their social identity as they become increasingly aware of their ego state. The theory states that the final stage of development is the genital stage from the age of 12 onwards, when Freud proposes that males and females become increasingly aware of their adult reproductive capabilities.

Freud's theory introduces the idea that human beings hold the potential for fixated behaviour. This means that an individual could become negatively confined to a particular stage (or stages) of development. As an example, if an infant experienced the trauma of losing its mother at the age of one, there is the possibility of this individual developing what Freud terms an 'oral fixation'. This fixated behaviour expresses itself at a later age through consciously chosen behaviour exemplified by the oral fixation of alcoholism. What makes the theory so original is that it is claimed that the conscious choice of behaviour has its origins in the repressed depths of the unconscious mind. Proponents of the theory claim that this repression can be released through psychodynamic counselling. This counselling may be needed in a situation when the individual has experienced a physical and/or emotional crisis during their development.

Crises leading to fixated behaviour can occur at any stage of development. According to Freud, this personal development directs the individual in the direction of one of two forces, either towards 'Thanatos' or 'Eros'. Eros, the Greek god of love, is interpreted by Freudians as contributing to an individual's optimism. Thanatos, the Greek personification of death, is perceived as contributing to an individual's sense of pessimism. How one develops determines whether one's conscious frame of mind directs the individual to the good or otherwise. It can be argued that Freud's legacy is to have left one of the most influential psychological theories to contribute to the discipline. It is, however, important to recognize that just because the theory is famous does not mean it is correct. This point will be developed later in the chapter.

In applying psychodynamic theory to classroom management, it is interesting to consider those learners who are alienated by the learning process, but no satisfactory explanation can be given as to why they have become so removed from learning. Freudian theory can be developed to suggest that these learners may have negative feelings within their subconscious minds. These negative feelings may be addressed through psychodynamic counselling. This counselling process is designed to ensure that the individual is able to reconcile the workings of both the conscious and unconscious mind. This is a way of applying psychodynamic psychology to classroom management. The wider supporting team within 'educare' (including counsellors and psychologists) may be able to support the learning process by giving potential explanations for why some learners find it difficult to cope with classroom environment.

Cognitive theory

Cognitive psychology can be understood as being a branch of psychology that is interested in what happens after a stimulus but before a response. It is a school of psychology that has become associated with the work of Jean Piaget and Lev Vygotsky. Malim and Birch (1998: 27) argue that Piaget is 'the most significant figure in the study of cognitive development'. Piaget's model of cognitive development has become particularly influential within psychology. According to Piaget, the human mind develops over time as an individual is stimulated by his/her surroundings. From the ages of zero to two, the child has basic thoughts or 'schemata'. Piaget claims that these initial thoughts are limited and instinctive. A baby has a 'crying schema', a 'grasping schema' and a 'feeding schema'. These thought processes develop from the age of two as the infant becomes capable of speech and develops what Piaget phrases as 'symbolic thought'. It is also proposed that between the ages of two and seven the child's problem-solving skills are limited because of two terms Piaget phrases as 'centration' and 'egocentricism'. By 'centration', Piaget means that the child can see one aspect of a situation's reality but not the total picture. As an example, a child between the ages of two and seven may think that a ton of lead is heavier than a ton of feathers because they 'centrate' or focus on one aspect of the problem. The child assumes that lead is a metal and therefore heavier than 'fluffy' feathers. This means that the child may not see that in fact both quantities are the same weight. By 'egocentrism' Piaget means that a child cannot see the true nature of a problem because problem solving occurs in relation to what the child knows about reality. As an example, if a child aged two to seven is asked what noise a reindeer makes they may say 'clip clop' instead of 'I don't know'. This is due to egocentrism. The child thinks that the reindeer looks like a horse and knows that a horse makes a 'clip clop' sound, so the child assumes that reindeer also make a 'clip clop' sound. Piaget claims that in order to progress through this stage of development the child needs to interact with its environment through play.

As a consequence of linguistic development, the infant becomes capable of more complex thought so that by the age of seven the preoperational stage has ended and the child is able to complete complex problem solving. This stage of development is phrased 'concrete operations'. This is because Piaget claims that children aged between 7 and 11 need to use props if they are to complete problem-solving activities. From 7 to 11 a child can calculate that three apples + two apples add up to make five apples, but Piaget claims that the child needs to have the actual apples in hand in order to complete the calculation. As this interaction occurs, the child will develop what Piaget phrases as 'reversible thinking'. This is the final stage of cognitive development occurring around 11 years of age. Once reversible thought has been reached, it is possible to problem solve within the mind, without using the props that a seven-year-old child needs. When one can apply reversible thinking to solving a problem, it means that one can see within one's mind that three + two is the same as seven − two.

Lev Vygotsky's work is seen as complementing Piaget's theory as opposed to being a radically different cognitive perspective (Malim and Birch, 1998: 469). Vygotsky places more emphasis upon the social factors influencing the child's cognitive development. One of Vygotsky's central ideas is the notion of each individual having a 'scaffold' of persons aiding their cognitive development. According to the nature of the scaffold, the individual's cognitive development is affected in either negative or positive ways. If, for example, the individual's peers are interested in academic issues, this social scaffold will impact upon cognitive development and make the individual more academic. If the opposite situation occurs, it leads to negative cognitive development. It can be argued that this theory complements Piaget's work because it explains why some students are 'late developers' and reach the stage of reversible thought beyond the age of 11. Vygotsky uses the term 'ZPD' or 'Zone of Proximal Development' to refer to when an individual has fulfilled their cognitive potential. This stage of development may occur at 11. It may occur beyond the age of 11. What becomes critical is the influence of one's cognitive development in relation to the 'scaffold' of individuals influencing one's cognitive development.

The idea of 'scaffolding' is very useful for classroom management. It is a concept that justifies the use of 'group work' within learning. Learning is viewed by Vygotsky as a 'social process'. It can be argued that dividing learners into suitable groups and facilitating appropriate problem-solving activities is likely to enhance classroom management. Reece and Walker (2007) encourage the notion of getting students to learn by 'doing' as soon as possible within teaching sessions. If this idea is considered in respect of Vygotsky's theory of social learning, there is the possibility of developing learning and teaching methods that both interest and motivate students.

Biological psychology

It can be argued that biological psychology is becoming of increasing importance due to the recent scientific advances, in particular, in relation to understanding human genetics. The biological perspective places an emphasis on the link between the thoughts of individuals and their hormonal and chromosomal composition. It is accepted by the scientific community that males and females differ in one pair of chromosomes and that before the infant is born the presence of a 'Y' chromosome leads to the development of testes. This in turn leads to the production of the hormone testosterone. As a consequence, males produce more androgens whereas females produce oestrogen and progesterone. Biologists such as Milton Diamond (1980) and Roger Gorski, McLean-Evans and Whalen (1966) emphasize the importance of biology in producing thoughts. It has been discovered that the male brain is physically different to the female brain due to the influence of the hormone testosterone. According to this theory, the inevitable consequence is that the thoughts occurring within the mind must have some biological basis and that differences in thought patterns are crucially linked to hormonal and chromosomal factors.

Biological psychology can help to explain why certain learners are able to accomplish particular learning tasks. 'Mature' students who are physically older than adolescent students may find that their thinking processes are able to cope with the learning process. In comparison, some adolescent learners may need to mature biologically before they can cope with aspects of the learning process. This means that if learning activities are adapted according to the specific biological needs of the learners this can be a means of improving classroom management.

Exploring how psychology can be applied to classroom management

The point has been made already that all of the psychological perspectives that have been introduced within this chapter are relevant for classroom management. There are a number of ways of applying the ideas from each psychological school to classroom management in order to improve and enhance professional practice. Moreover, if the ideas are combined they offer the potential to apply holistic ideas to managing behaviour in order to assist learners with complex needs. This next section of the chapter reflects on some of the ways that these ideas can be applied by the Lifelong Learning Sector.

Behaviourism and classroom management

One of the most well-known behaviourist therapies is called 'token economy'. The therapy is based on the principle of conditioning responses, effectively manipulating choice so that positive behaviour occurs. Most children have complex thoughts, and they are likely to choose whether to conform with or rebel against accepted social requirements. This acceptance or rebellion can be overt and explicit or implicit and assumed. Token economy attempts to produce conformity of response. At the end of every day in which the individual has complied with what is required, a reward or 'token' is offered. This token has to have appeal and value to the person receiving the therapy. If there is a lack of compliance with the programme, the token is denied. After a short period of time, for example, five days of compliance, the recipient is rewarded with a bigger treat or prize. Token economy is used within many educational contexts. It can represent a behaviourist attempt to get learners to comply with what is required of them within the learning environment. It is a therapy that is also used within other professional contexts such as 'Early Years', but as we shall see later in the chapter, it is a therapy that is not without its critics.

Another therapy that is available for the Lifelong Learning Sector is biofeedback. This therapy may be used with learners who have been referred for professional help because they are highly anxious. Music, light, aroma and relaxing furnishings are combined to produce an environment that can physically relax the individual. The therapy is essentially attempting to produce relaxing thoughts within the learner's mind by manipulating external variables.

A third popular therapy that has its origins within behaviourist theory is known as 'systematic desensitization'. This therapy may be used with learners who have phobias. The learner is made to come to terms with his/her phobia in a controlled environment. It is proposed that as a result of gradually exposing the child to the phobia in a non-threatening way, the phobic object becomes manageable and increasingly less debilitating. Once again the emphasis is placed upon the importance of manipulating the individual's thoughts in order to produce positive ways of thinking about the phobia. The following case-study example outlines the ways in which behaviourism can be applied to the Lifelong Learning Sector. It also reveals some of the potential difficulties that exist when particular therapies are applied to learners with particular needs.

Case Study

Peter is 14 and has learning disabilities, but there has been no definitive diagnosis of the nature of his disability. He is thought to have a combination of autism and learning disability. Peter has recently started attending music lessons at his local College. When Peter is in College, he has a habit of tearing paper from books during the teaching sessions. In an attempt to get Peter to change his behaviour, a token economy programme has been designed by the members of the multidisciplinary team who work with him. Peter loves listening to music, and the token economy programme involves giving Peter a token on each day when he has not torn paper from the learning resources that are being used. Peter likes chocolate and when he has complied with the token economy programme he is given a chocolate treat of his choice. If he does not follow what is expected of him, Peter is denied this reward. Upon receiving five tokens, Peter is given the opportunity to listen to a music DVD of his choice. Some of the College staff working with Peter have expressed concerns that there are ethical problems with this behaviour modification programme. There are concerns that this conditioning violates Peter's right to choose what he should and should not do.

Humanist therapies

The humanist philosophy of Carl Rogers is at the centre of what is deemed as being 'good practice' within facilitative learning. Rogers proposes an egalitarian model of practice in which the teacher is not aloof from the learner but 'with' the learner. Empathy is a particularly important aspect of the Rogerian way. The teacher must be there for the learner and prepared to be genuine and assertive. According to Rogers, a teacher who is 'genuine' can enable the learner's personal growth and development.

Effective practice is facilitated upon resolving the 'would/should dilemma'. Rogers considers that this dilemma is the cause of anxiety that in turn prevents individual development.

Teachers should also direct learners to their 'beautiful inner self'. Rogers believes that all individuals are innately good and that it is only the tension that results from a would/should dilemma that makes the individual a less than good person. Through a genuine and empathetic relationship, it is postulated that the would/should dilemma will be replaced by an assertive awareness of one's inner goodness. Although there are many applications for these ideas, the generalizing assumptions that are made within humanism can mean that its application is restricted. This argument is exemplified in the following case-study example and in the final section of the chapter.

Case Study

Julie has recently qualified as a lecturer in sociology, and she is working with learners aged 16 to 18 in an inner city FE College. Within the last few months, there has been an escalation of racial tension between black and white youths. The situation is further complicated by an outbreak of violence between Asian and Afro-Caribbean youths. As a student, Julie was inspired by the ideas of Carl Rogers during a 'Promoting Positive Behaviour' module, and she bases her teaching approach upon the principles of client-centred therapy. Within one of her first teaching sessions with an Asian student, Julie is devastated when the student runs out of the classroom during a lecture about 'models of sociological thought'. Julie realises that her values are very different from the values of this student and that this limits the application of client-centred teaching. In the past she has found that this approach to learning and teaching works with white learners who seem to share many of her values, but it is an altogether different challenge applying these ideas in this particular context.

Psychodynamic therapies

The psychodynamic model of the mind holds that conscious thoughts are influenced by the unconscious mind. This means that therapy involves releasing what is being unconsciously repressed. This then enables the individual to deal with these thoughts within the conscious mind. The psychodynamic therapist is responsible for interpreting what is within the individual's unconscious mind by analysing dreams and/or using hypnotherapy. Dream and fantasy analysis become a means of interpreting what is being repressed. It is considered to be imperative for repressed unconscious thoughts to be released into the conscious mind in order to lessen the effects of repression. The Freudian model holds that fixated behaviour has its basis in repression so that the critical role of the therapist is one of releasing repressed thoughts and then recommending ways of consciously dealing with these thoughts.

The psychodynamic model is hierarchical as opposed to being equalitarian. The omniscient therapist is in a position of power over his/her clients, a characteristic that can be deemed as being opposed to the equalitarian approach of Carl Rogers. This has consequences for the situations in which the therapy can be used and the learners upon whom the therapy should be used. This critique of psychodynamic therapy is exemplified in the subsequent case study.

Case Study

Daniel is 15 and he has not attended school for over five months because he suffers from 'panic attacks'. He does not know why he experiences these panic attacks, but he says that whenever he thinks about going to school he is unable to eat and that he has 'butterflies' in his stomach. Since there is no conscious explanation for his panic attacks, Daniel's psychiatrist has recommended a number of hypnotherapy sessions in order to identify if there is an unconscious repressed reason for Daniel's behaviour. Under hypnosis, Daniel talks about his anxieties about school, in particular his fear of some of the other pupils and of a recent incident when an older boy physically assaulted him in the school yard. Daniel had never disclosed this incident to anyone before, and this was thought to be a major benefit of the hypnotherapy sessions. When Daniel was asked about this incident after his hypno- therapy had finished, he said that this was not the main reason for his fear of school and that he still did not know why he was having his panic attacks. This was a difficulty of the hypnotherapy sessions. Although it did appear to shed light on some of the things that Daniel was repressing, it still did not explain a reason for the panic attacks that both Daniel and his psychiatrist could unanimously agree upon. Daniel's psychiatrist said that he thought Daniel was having panic attacks because he was afraid of being bullied, but Daniel denied this and said he did not know what was causing the anxiety.

Cognitive therapies

Cognitive psychologists emphasize the importance of studying what happens after a stimulus but before a reaction. They are interested in the cognitive processes that produce thoughts within the mind. It is proposed that through manipulating these cognitive processes one's thought processes can change. If, for example, a student is unable to control their anger, it may be possible to apply cognitive therapy so that this anger is effectively managed. By counselling the individual to consciously change the thought processes occurring within the mind so that they think differently, there follows a cognitive restructuring. This allows the individual to think about the world in a different way. It is a therapy relying on psychological techniques as opposed to a medical therapy. If it is combined with other psychological therapies, it can offer a potential solution to various psychological problems, such as low self-esteem and inability to manage anger. The following case-study example outlines how cognitive therapy can be applied to a particular example of anger management.

Case Study

Taylor is 18 and comes from a travelling family who have recently settled into the local community. He has a younger brother who is 15, but his father has left the family home. Taylor is becoming increas- ingly prone to violent outbursts. It appears that he gradually becomes angry and then attacks his mother, his brother or both. Taylor's mother has become very concerned about these outbursts. In a recent incident during an 'Entry to Education' session at his local College, Taylor screamed at another

⇨

student that he was going to 'strangle' him, and Taylor's College tutor has admitted that it is a 'challenge' to include him within the formal educational system. The family have been helped by social services, and Taylor's social worker referred the child to a cognitive behaviourist therapist who began to counsel Taylor. The therapy seemed to have some success when Taylor and his mother attended the sessions. It was explained to Taylor's mother that she must always maintain control of the situation when Taylor was having these outbursts by thinking in a non-aggressive and assertive way. When Taylor was having an aggressive outburst, he had to be isolated from his mother and his sister. Taylor's mother was told that she should go and see Taylor at five-minute intervals to ask if he had 'calmed down' so that Taylor would learn that a consistent strategy was in place to deal with his violent outbursts. The combination of anger management and applied behaviourism seemed to make a significant difference in controlling Taylor's violent outbursts.

Reflection

It is likely that most teachers will have experienced educational situations that have required some form of 'anger management' from students, parents, staff or all three!! The advantage of attempting the cognitive structuring that is highlighted in the above case study is that it is attempting to deal with the situation in an assertive 'win-win' way. The application of cognitive therapy is also being used in an attempt to be as inclusive as possible. This is because the complex needs of an unorthodox learner are being acknowledged as opposed to the learner being 'excluded' from the educational system.

Biological therapies

Biological psychology attempts to understand the human mind by applying traditional western scientific principles. Therapies are based on the idea that thought processes are determined by the genetic and hormonal nature of the brain. It is also proposed that thought processes can be influenced by drug therapy. As an example, an overly aggressive individual may be diagnosed as being overly aggressive because of the presence of too much testosterone within the body. This male hormone may need to be regulated by medication that lessens the aggressive impulses that are produced within the mind.

In the application of therapies based upon biological psychology, tutors in the Lifelong Learning Sector may be required to be aware of the legitimate (!) drug therapy of particular learners. To give an example, it has been discovered that in some instances placing the individual on a drug regime based on dopamine can regulate schizophrenia. If levels of dopamine within the brain determine the presence or otherwise of schizophrenic tendencies, it can be argued that drug therapies have their value. It may also be argued that the precise link between the chemical composition of the brain and 'thought processes' has never been exactly established and that this psychological perspective has not developed as yet to the extent that it can offer every possible solution for every possible psychological need.

Activity 4.4

Think about each of the schools of psychology outlined in Table 4.1 and suggest how they might explain why learners are unable to cope with a classroom environment.

Feedback

Each of the psychological schools of thought would answer the question differently. Behaviourist psychologists think that the external environment shapes the individual. This means that 'being unable to cope with the classroom environment' would be regarded as being a form of learned behaviour. It is proposed that the way to change the behaviour is through systems of reward and punishment that encourage the formation of a positive view of learning within a classroom environment. Humanists such as Carl Rogers would interpret this form of 'challenging behaviour' as a sign of anxiety. Anxiety is a product of what Rogers describes as a 'would/should' dilemma; in other words, an individual is not able to do what they would like to do. Resolve this dilemma and they are less likely to be unwilling to learn in a classroom environment. Psychoanalysts consider that conscious thoughts are influenced by what is within the unconscious mind. Negative feelings about the classroom environment may be considered to be a conscious fixation resulting from a repressed unconscious experience. It may be postulated that when the individual was an infant they had a traumatic experience during one of their developmental stages and that the conscious act of 'being unable to cope with the classroom environment' is a means of releasing this repressed thought. The way to resolve this fixation is to have psychodynamic counselling whereby the counsellor can help the individual to resolve the conflict between unconscious and conscious thoughts. Neurobiological psychologists explain behaviour through analysing an individual's genetic composition. The implication is that being unable to cope with conventional learning environments has a biological basis. The way to make progress in rectifying this 'problem' behaviour is to isolate and amend the biological gene promoting this negative reaction. At present, this procedure is talked about as opposed to being done. Cognitive psychologists would explain the behaviour as being part of an individual's cognitive map or thinking processes. It is a type of behaviour that comes from within the mind. In order to stop individuals having a negative perception of the classroom environment, it may be proposed that the individual needs to have a cognitive restructuring of their thinking processes via cognitive counselling.

Activity 4.5

When you are next teaching, begin a research diary and make a note of which psychological therapies are being applied by the staff you work with. Analyse the effectiveness of the therapies by identifying which therapies work and why you think they are working. Make sure that you respect principles of confidentiality!

We can now complete the chapter by focusing our discussion on critically appraising the psychological perspectives in respect of the value they have for classroom management in the Lifelong Learning Sector.

Critical appraisal of how psychological therapies can be used by the Lifelong Learning Sector

There is no single perspective that holds all the answers to solving the challenges of classroom management. This means that the psychological therapies that have been outlined have limitations if they are applied in isolation.

Appraising behaviourist contributions to classroom management

The behaviourist therapies that have been summarized can make the mistake of focusing upon external variables to such an extent that the particular needs of individuals are not met. Every human being does not react in the same way to an external response. Even complex mammals such as dolphins can defy the laws of operant conditioning by doing the opposite to what they are expected to do. This means that there can be no scientific certainty of the therapies that are informed by this perspective. There is a further difficulty with behaviourist therapies that may be summarized as being linked to the unique nature of the human mind. There are profound ethical difficulties with therapies such as token economy. It can be claimed that token economy programmes may not respect dignity and human rights. A token economy programme is essentially saying, 'Do this for me and you will be rewarded.' This is a power relationship, and it could be argued that the learner is being manipulated in hierarchical non-egalitarian ways. This means that there are critiques of behaviourist therapies and concerns that they have limited application to classroom management. It leads Malim and Birch (1998: 24) to criticize behaviourist therapies because they can be 'mechanistic' and that they 'overlook the realm of consciousness and subjective experience'.

Appraising humanism

It can also be proposed that there are limitations in the application of Rogerian client-centred therapy. If a learner is to accept the importance of resolving the would/should dilemma, it is important that they share similar values to those of the teacher. The learner needs to accept that the values of the teacher are important so that there can be a situation where there is a link between what both the teacher and learner want to achieve. There are, however, many instances when the values of the child may be opposed to the values of the teacher. This can be exemplified within a school environment in which the pupils do not want to achieve what their teachers perceive as being important. This is supported by research that has been completed on the 'chava' subculture within the north-east of England. It is also acknowledged by Anne Watson (2004) in her discussion of the failings of the wider academic curriculum within the United Kingdom. Watson argues that it is not so much that the curriculum is a 'bad idea'; it is more that there is little awareness of how to unite the values of the learners and their teachers. This can mean that if a teacher in the Lifelong Learning Sector is to attempt to apply the philosophy of Rogers the ideas cannot work because there is no common under-standing of what is important and achievable. It is all very well to say that a would/should dilemma should be resolved, but a learner can only be directed to their 'inner beautiful self' if they perceive that self through a shared sense of identity with their teacher. Malim and Birch (1998: 803) develop this criticism by arguing that a critical limitation with humanist therapies relates to the assumption that 'self-actualization' is a principal human motivation. Self-actualization may motivate particular groups of individuals, but it cannot be assumed to be a universal characteristic of every human being at every point in time.

Appraising psychodynamic theory

It may be argued that psychodynamic therapy has as many limitations as uses. The model is not based upon a sound methodology, and many of the theoretical ideas can be challenged. It is a theory that is built upon assumptions of how the mind operates. If this is the case, it can be argued that any successes within psychodynamic theory are due to good fortune as much as anything else. A more significant critique of psychodynamic therapy is that it is a theory that is laden with negative value assumptions. The therapist is perceived to be in control of interpreting the individual's problems. The classic image of the psychiatric couch can be applied to psychodynamic theory. This means that there is no equality of dialogue. As opposed to influencing the therapeutic process, the individual is effectively disempowered by a therapist who tells 'what should be done' in order to resolve 'fixated behaviour'. Malim and Birch (1998: 802) reinforce this criticism by emphasizing that within psychoanalytical therapies there are problems of 'validation'. It may be suggested that within psychodynamic therapy the truth is invented as opposed to being truth in itself.

Appraising cognitive theory

The cognitive psychology of Jean Piaget can also be criticized. It is a theory that may have been mistranslated and turned into an unworkable model of the mind. Can it be accepted that the human brain moves through the stages that have become accepted as integral to Piaget's model? If not and if thoughts develop through more of a process than the movement through distinct stages of development, it means that the potential application of cognitive therapy is called into question. A further criticism is that although one can take apart a computer and identify the microchips making up its component parts, the human brain is altogether more complex. All sorts of factors that are not necessarily conscious inform cognitive processes. This may mean that a perspective that focuses upon what happens after a stimulus but before a response is dealing with part of the picture but not the whole picture of human thought. A further criticism of cognitive therapy is that the learner's problem behaviours or thoughts are always changed to those that the therapist sees as being acceptable. Malim and Birch (1998: 801) question whether it can always be the case that the therapist has the correct perspective on the world and that the child's cognitive outlook is in need of total change.

Appraising biological psychology

The biological therapies that are available to learners may be criticized because of what we do not know as opposed to what we do know. There is still much work that needs to be done in order to understand the hormonal and genetic composition of the brain. There is also a degree of uncertainty as to why some chemical treatments work with some individuals and yet the same treatments are less effective in another identical context. This anxiety can be combined with the concern existing over the side effects of drug-based therapy and the ethical implications this has for learners. Taking a particular pill might make someone less aggressive, but if the consequences are the docility exemplified in 'One Flew Over the Cuckoo's Nest' this effectively reduces the individual's life chances. There is also the critique that biological psychology is reductionist. It reduces the complex functioning of the brain to the relationship existing between genes, chromosomes and hormones. By concentrating the focus on this single area, it can be argued that there is a possibility that other variables influencing human thought and behaviour are overlooked.

Summary of key points

In this opening chapter, psychology has been applied to classroom management in the Lifelong Learning Sector. We have proposed that psychology is a complex discipline with competing views on how the subject ought to be studied. It is a diverse discipline with a range of identifiable 'sub-areas' of interest. There are a number of schools of psychology, each of which has adopted its own model of the person. The chapter has defined and explored five major perspectives that are of use to teachers in the Lifelong Learning Sector for classroom management. Examples of specific applications of theory to practice have been provided, and there has been a critical appraisal of each of the theories. It may be argued that the best way to apply psychology to classroom management is to combine the perspectives and their ideas in such a way that the complex learning needs of individuals are more likely to be met. If this is done, it produces an holistic approach to meeting individual needs. This helps to apply the ideas of Wallace (2007) in managing behaviour within the Lifelong Learning Sector. If these psychological ideas are combined with other perspectives from social science such as counselling, there is the further likelihood that our understanding of classroom management can be enhanced. It may be argued that this is the best way to apply psychology to classroom management.

This chapter links to the following SVUK professional standards:

Professional values

AS 4: Reflection and evaluation of their own practice and their continuing professional development as teachers.
AS 7: Improving the quality of their practice.

Professional Knowledge and Understanding

AK 1.1: What motivates learners to learn and the importance of learners' experience and aspirations.
AK 3.1: Issues of equality, diversity and inclusion.
AK 4.1: Principles, frameworks and theories which underpin good practice in learning and teaching.
AK 4.2: The impact of own practice on individuals and their learning.
AK 4.3: Ways to reflect, evaluate and use research to develop own practice and to share good practice with others.
AK 5.1: Ways to communicate and collaborate with colleagues and/or others to enhance learners' experience.

Professional practice

AP 4.2: Reflect on and demonstrate commitment to improvement of own personal and teaching skills through regular evaluation and use of feedback.
AP 4.3: Share good practice with others and engage in continuing professional development through reflection, evaluation and appropriate use of research.
AP 7.3: Use feedback to develop own practice within the organization's systems.

Self-assessment questions

Question 1: What are the five major schools of psychology?
Question 2: How can teachers in the Lifelong Learning Sector apply the schools of psychology to classroom management in order to help children to maximize their professional practice?
Question 3: Give an example of strength and weakness of each of the psychological schools of thought in respect of classroom management.

Moving on feature

This chapter has introduced applying psychology to classroom management. Chapter 5 introduces you to a number of different educational contexts within the Lifelong Learning

Sector. Try to think of how the material in this chapter can be applied to managing behaviour within different educational contexts in order to meet the needs of a variety of learners.

Further reading

Wallace, S. (2007a), *Managing Behaviour in the Lifelong Learning Sector*. Exeter: Learning Matters.

An excellent textbook in terms of complementing the material in this chapter and relevance to the Lifelong Learning Sector.

Malim, T. and Birch, A. (1998), *Introductory Psychology*. London: Palgrave Macmillan.

An excellent textbook that is written in an accessible way and makes clear links to applying theory to practice.

References

Audi, R. (1995), *The Cambridge Dictionary of Philosophy*. Cambridge: Cambridge University Press.

Diamond, M. (1980), *Sexual Decisions*. London: Little Brown.

Gorski, R., McLean-Evans, H. and Whalen, R. (1966), *The Brain and Gonadal Function*. California: University of California Press.

Gross, R. D. (2001), *Psychology: The Science of Mind and Behaviour*. London: Hodder Arnold H&S.

Kohler, W. (1927), *The Mentality of Apes*. London: Kegan Paul.

Lucas, N. (2007), 'The in-service training of adult literacy, numeracy and English for speakers of other languages teachers in England; the challenges of a "standards-led model"'. *Journal of In-Service Education*, 3, 125-142.

Malim, T. and Birch, A. (1998), *Introductory Psychology*. London: Palgrave Macmillan.

Reece, I. and Walker, S. (2007), *Teaching Training and Learning: A Practical Guide*. Sunderland: Business Education Publishers.

Online dictionary. Online: *www.dictionary.reference.com*

Wallace, S. (2007), *Teaching Tutoring and Training in the Lifelong Learning Sector*. Exeter: Learning Matters.

Watson, A. (2004), 'Reconfiguring the public sphere: implications for analyses of educational policy'. *British Journal of Educational Studies*, 52(3): 228–248.

5 Curriculum Development for Inclusive Practice

Chapter Outline

Learning Outcomes

After reading this chapter you should be able to

- define the terms 'widening participation', 'curriculum', 'inclusion' and 'inclusive practice' within the parameters of learning and teaching in Lifelong Learning settings;
- understand and evaluate some of the ways that the curriculum can be developed to promote inclusive practices;
- critically appraise the scope and potential limitations of developing the curriculum to promote inclusive practices within Lifelong Learning settings.

Introduction

This chapter considers key factors in learning and teaching for the Lifelong Learning sector – the concepts 'curriculum', 'widening participation', 'inclusion' and 'inclusive practice' The chapter will attempt to

suggest some defining characteristics of the curriculum and inclusive practice;
explore issues associated with widening participation and inclusion;
explore some of the dilemmas facing you, as a trainee teacher, when you are planning, designing, implementing and reviewing a curriculum to support inclusive practice.

The overarching aim of the chapter is to assist you in drawing your own conclusions regarding curriculum development for inclusive practice when applied to your own teaching.

Throughout the chapter, there are formative activities that reinforce learning in relation to curriculum and inclusive practice that are of relevance for the Lifelong Learning Sector. The chapter explores a range of key issues for the trainee teacher to consider in designing an inclusive curriculum, some of which are as follows:

defining 'curriculum' 'widening participation', 'inclusion' and 'inclusive practices' and their relationship to 'curriculum development' for inclusive practice;
implementing, reviewing, evaluating and adapting the curriculum to promote inclusive practice;
equality and diversity – ethical and legal issues;
equality and diversity – curriculum design for inclusive practice.

Defining 'curriculum', 'widening participation' and 'inclusion'

Activity 5.1

What is your understanding of the terms 'curriculum', 'widening participation' and 'inclusion'?

Feedback

This part of the chapter will focus upon defining these key terms and their use within educational contexts; the chapter will then go on to explore the influences of these on the development, delivery and review of an inclusive curriculum.

The Oxford English Dictionary (OED) defines the curriculum in the following way: *A course; specifically, a regular course of study or training, as at school or university.* Kelly (1995: 5) defines the term curriculum as '*All the learning which is planned and guided, whether carried on in groups or*

⇨

individually'. In simplistic terms, the curriculum can therefore be defined as a course of planned or guided learning completed on an individual basis or in groups.

An excellent example of a preset curriculum currently in use is the *Adult Literacy Core Curriculum (2001)*. This is a curriculum framework for planning programmes of learning for adults with literacy and communication difficulties. It is set at five different levels (Entry Level 1, Entry Level 2, Entry Level 3, Level 1 and Level 2), and at each level the curriculum includes aims and objectives for learning at text, sentence and word level. The framework also has criteria for measuring learning progression and example activities that practitioners can use in their own teaching practices.

Widening Participation first became a major focus of attention for Further Education Colleges with the publication of *Learning Works written by Helena Kennedy Q. C. in June 1997. This paper was developed in response to the Further Education Funding Council's (FEFC) drive to promote access to further education for people who do not participate in education and training but who could benefit from it* (FEFC, 1997: 3).

For further education colleges, this publication became a major influence in the programmes of study offered by colleges, as this led to a streamlining of funding that 'responded' to the widening participation agenda. In other words, there has been a focus on the recruitment of 'unrepresented groups' as defined in FEFC funding council criteria. This put widening participation firmly at the centre of further education training, and this is still the case in the present day. This has led to Further Education Colleges, who are primarily funded by their local Learning and Skills Council (LSC), having funding for widening participation calculated into their yearly funding allowance. Therefore, it is in a FE college's best interest to be actively engaged in the widening participation agenda. It is also worth mentioning Higher Education Institution (HEI) Funding for widening participation as FE colleges now frequently work with HEIs in partnership to deliver HE programmes in an FE environment. HEIs work within the Higher Education Funding Council for England's Strategic Plan (2009–2011) and aspects of this plan relate to the widening participation agenda. HEIs have to demonstrate that they are providing ongoing opportunities for different social groups and under-represented groups to access higher education, specifically disabled students, mature students, women and men and all ethnic groups whether they are physically attending university or college sites. Colleges and HEIs can demonstrate this via analysis of statistical data taken from student enrolment information, for example, gender, age, ethnicity, residential address and a whole range of other relevant information can be taken and analysed for participation trends over set amounts of time and presented as evidence. In summary, widening participation can be considered to be an aspect of inclusion that discusses not how someone can be included in a learning situation' in the classroom' but the more fundamental aspect of 'who' should be included in participating in learning (or the curriculum) and why. Ongoing key external drivers attempt to ensure that the student body will continue to be diverse, and with this diversity ideally arrives a range of differing needs that need to be met both at organisational and curriculum level.

How is the term 'inclusion' defined? The OED online provides a useful definition of inclusion, which is *the act of Including or the state of being included*. This suggests that inclusion is primarily about positioning a learner with particular needs in a mainstream class so that they are included in that learning situation.

The act of inclusion also suggests some activity or 'action' to ensure inclusion can take place; for example, inclusion can also be about the removal of physical barriers that prevent access, for example, providing a ramp for wheelchair users to access a building. Inclusion may also lead to the provision of funds to learners from socially disadvantaged background so that they attend a programme of learning. Some of these actions may encourage widening participation and inclusion, in terms of physical, financial, and to some extent religious barrier removal, but how far do these activities support 'inclusion' in terms of equality of opportunity to access learning in the classroom or 'inclusive practice'? The following section of this chapter will explore this theme in detail.

Curriculum design and implementation for inclusive practice

Activity 5.2

By now you will be familiar with the process of planning a curriculum for delivery and will have highlighted some of the constraints and issues around this. What you may not have done is thought in-depth about some of the more specific needs that individual learners may have within these groups. Take some time to reflect on what these needs might be when planning a curriculum for the following groups of students that promotes inclusion and make a note of how their particular needs may impact further upon your planning:

- 14-to 16-year-old students in both school settings and college settings,
- mainstream FE groups, aged 16–19,
- adult learners in community settings from disadvantaged backgrounds,
- students with significant learning difficulties and disabilities,
- apprentices on day release,
- adults learning for pleasure on a recreational basis,
- higher education students studying in colleges of further education,
- students on professional courses for continuing professional development.

Feedback

Tomlinson (1996) defines inclusive learning as the greatest degree of match or fit between how learners learn best, what they need and want to learn, and what is required of the sector, a college and teachers for successful learning to take place (Gravells and Simpson, 2009: 34). Tummons (2009: 94) argues that 'inclusive practice' is thinking about our teaching, and our curricula, in such a way that any student can access it to the best of their potential ability.

Petty (2004) discusses differentiation along similar lines and defines it as adopting strategies that ensure success in learning for all, by accommodating individual differences of any kind. These definitions range from 13 years ago to the present day – but all have one key fundamental theme, which is that in order to provide the best opportunities for learning to take place we must be flexible and adapt our teaching practices accordingly. In summary, 'inclusive practice' can be defined as 'the use of a variety of differentiated approaches to teaching and learning in the classroom in order to deliver the curricula content in such a way as to promote as wider access to learning for as many learners as possible.

If we look at the previous definitions of inclusive practice and think further about their implications for curriculum development, a key related area for consideration is differentiation. You will often find inclusion and differentiation discussed together because inclusive learning process links to differentiated teaching and learning practices. So what is a differentiated classroom? This has been described by Tomlinson (2001: 1) as a classroom which *provides different avenues to acquiring content, to processing or making sense of ideas and to developing products so that each student can learn effectively.* Tomlinson (1997) then goes on to discuss the advantages of a differentiated classroom as it provides the best access to learning, promotes effectiveness of learning and encourages motivation in learning. Tomlinson's (1997) notion of a differentiated classroom emphasizes that learning experiences need to be based upon readiness to learn, learning interests and learning profiles. This means that the content and activities in the session and the expected learning outcomes are developed according to the varied needs of the group and the individual learners. The consequences are that teaching and learning activities are focused on key concepts of learning so that teachers and students work together to ensure that learners are challenged and continually engaged in learning. Some of Tomlinson's (1997) teaching and learning strategies to promote a differentiated learning experience for the learners are summarized as follows:

> The teacher should coordinate the use of time, space and activities.
> There should be flexible grouping which ensures fluidity of working arrangements that are consistent as far as possible.
> This should include a range of strategies, such as whole class learning, paired learning, small group learning, teacher-selected learning groups and random learning groups.
> Flexible use of time is needed to respond to the learners' needs at any given time.

A wide variety of classroom management strategies are needed, such as independent study, interest groups, learning buddies and tiered assignments in order to help to target instruction to the students' needs. There should be clear criteria for success developed at both group and individual level to provide guidance to the students as to what would be a successful learning outcome.

Formative and summative assessment activities should be varied to enable the learners to demonstrate their own thoughts and learning growth. These broader but important factors provide some theoretical parameters which guide the more practical aspects of planning for teaching and learning. This means that developing schemes of work and planning delivery are critical aspects of the curriculum process. As you will be aware by now, the fundamental areas for consideration when planning a scheme of work include

> the course content and overall aims of the course,
> the time constraints which the teacher has to work within,
> the best opportunities for learning and how learning is to be delivered,
> the type of knowledge and skills to be developed,
> the requirements of professional bodies/occupational standards,
> the methods to be adopted in order to measure to what extent learning has taken place,
> any specialist knowledge that is required to deliver the curriculum,
> the available physical and human resources must be considered in the planning.

The scheme of work is the framework document that is developed by teachers to help them to identify what is to be included in each individual session plan. Good session plans will include the relevant information from a scheme of work but will also be expanded to provide more detail of how particular sessions will be delivered. This may be the most appropriate point for teachers to consider the more specific detail and information that is required to deliver a truly inclusive curriculum. These may include, for example, specific details about the entry behaviour and individual needs of each learner, for example, levels of ability in literacy and numeracy.

As trainee teachers, when thinking about making the curriculum accessible, you need to consider all of the above and then move on one step further to think about the needs of your learners as individuals and how the curriculum can be planned to be as inclusive as possible. As we have discussed earlier in the chapter, a truly inclusive curriculum takes account of the needs of the learners in order for them to be provided with the best opportunities to learn.

According to Gravells and Simpson (2009) student teachers should be proactive at the planning stage in thinking about the wider implications for meeting the individual needs of the learners. This means that it is important to consider

> whether the physical learning environment provides any barriers to accessibility for learners and what can be done to address this;
> differentiated teaching and learning activities planned at both scheme of work and session planning level to ensure that all of the learners can access learning equally;
> making reference to a variety of cultures, religions and traditions;
> the diversity of your students.

As teachers, our primary concern should always be that we are enabling our learners to fulfil their full potential by providing them with the most appropriate learning opportunities possible. As indicated earlier in this chapter, FE colleges are effective at recruiting learners from a range of backgrounds at both further education and higher education level. Some typical examples of types of student groups, according to Tummons (2009: 93–94) are as follows: *14-to 16-year-old students in both school settings and college settings; mainstream FE groups, aged 16 to 19; adult learners in community settings, on either externally accredited programmes or on programmes where they are learning purely for pleasure and who may sometimes come from disadvantaged backgrounds; students with significant learning difficulties and/ or disabilities and apprentices on day release* . In addition to this, in the current educational climate, we have to consider higher education students studying in colleges of further education.

Although this indicates the relative success of the widening participation agenda, the very fact that colleges are recruiting learners from such diverse backgrounds brings a range of educational challenges that the teacher will have to consider when planning a curriculum that can be delivered in a truly inclusive way.

Let us consider the groups mentioned by Tummons and consider the needs they may have and how this might influence a teacher when planning the curriculum to ensure inclusive practice.

14- to 16-year-old students in both school settings and college settings

14- to 16-year-olds in colleges and schools can bring their own set of educational challenges. School age children who are attending programmes in FE can struggle with the academic curriculum, and a more vocationally based or practical curriculum may be more appropriate to their learning style, individual motivations and needs. If these learners demonstrate challenging forms of behaviour like refusing to participate in tasks or disrupting other learners, you will have to develop strategies and approaches to cope with this situation. This may include planning individual tasks for learners who demonstrate challenging behaviour or adapting the curriculum to enable it to meet the learners' needs more effectively. This range of strategies, some of which do not directly relate to the curriculum itself, may encourage and enable the learner to access the curriculum and gain as much as possible from the learning process.

Mainstream FE groups (16-to 19-year-olds) may appear to be a homogenous group of learners, and you may consider that differentiated approaches to practice are not an issue for a group of learners such as this. This is not necessarily the case as even large groups of mainstream learners need to be made to consider a range of curriculum strategies. One of these strategies may be the range of different learning styles that will be present in a classroom at any one time. There has been research carried out on learning styles, such as with the Visual, Auditory Kinaesthetic Module (VAK) that was developed by Fernald, Keller, Orton, Gillingham, Stillman and Montessori in the 1920s. The main thrust of this research is that learners need to be enabled to complete learning tasks in a way which best suits their needs. This means that some learners may be more visual and learn best from the use of visual diagrams rather than linear lists. Other learners prefer to complete practical activities in order to learn, and others may learn best by hearing something and then reciting the information. This research has summarized that learners will not necessarily fall neatly into one category and that learners are more likely to have a combination of preferred learning approaches, such as visual/kinaesthetic or auditory/visual. More recently Howard Gardner's (1993) 'multiple intelligences' categorize learners as having particular 'intelligences'. This means that a learner may be verbal/linguistic or musical/rhythmic or intrapersonal so that in theory teachers should adapt their teaching and learning approaches to meet these various needs. The work of Gardner has been criticized, with other educationalists such as Frank Coffield (2004) concluding that, in general, it is good teaching practice to use a range of teaching and learning strategies and that if this is done effectively all learners in the group will be able to access the curriculum.

What considerations should there be for practice and the inclusive curriculum?

If, for example, you use only electronic visual aids such as Microsoft PowerPoint and didactic teaching methods for the whole of the session, what about tactile learners, what about learners who learn best from social interaction and group work? Vygotsky (1978) argues that learning is a social activity and that social interaction plays a fundamental role in the development of cognition. The argument runs that for meaningful learning to take place, social interaction is necessary. A didactic approach to teaching can mean that learners are not fully engaged in the learning process. One might even argue that this means that an inclusive curriculum for all learners is not being provided. This is without considering the implications for learners in the session who may have hidden disabilities (see later in this chapter for a detailed discussion of legal issues around this area) that may require a variety of teaching and learning approaches to gain from the classroom experience.

Adult learners in community settings

This is possibly the most informal setting for teaching and learning to take place. The social and environmental barriers can be seen to be less than in a formal FE college setting, and the learning environment may be more relaxed and more appropriate for learners of this nature in order to facilitate learning. Though this may be the case, there are further considerations for learning and inclusive practices. These considerations can depend upon whether the learners are on externally accredited awards with all the inherent constraints outlined earlier or whether they are adults on courses for pleasure. Each will be discussed briefly within a well-known theory of how adults learn. This theory of adult learning is more commonly called andragogy. This term was first used by Alexander Kapp (1833) (a German educator) in 1833 and was developed into a theory of adult education by the American educator, Malcolm Knowles (1984) (in Tennant, 1997). This theory of adult learning relies on a range of assumptions about the way adults learn; the key main assumptions are that adults are self-directed, motivated learners who learn best when they have some autonomy over their learning approaches, have an interest in what they are studying and that social integration is a valuable part of the learning process. Motivation in itself is an important aspect of learning. Motivation can be seen to be intrinsic or extrinsic, and whether motivation is intrinsic or extrinsic in orientation can have an impact upon the success of learning. *Generally, intrinsic interest in a subject is associated with high levels of intrinsic motivation, and this in turn is linked to successful learning/achievement outcomes* (Brown, Armstrong and Thompson, 1989: 16). Extrinsic motivation is associated with factors outside or external to the person and can be seen to have a controlling aspect (Beck, 1990). Brown, Armstrong and Thompson (1989: 16) explains that *learners who are extrinsically motivated are influenced by external rewards and pressures. Learners who have high extrinsically motivating factors can feel 'controlled' by them, and this can have a negative impact on their intrinsic motivation.* Educationally, intrinsic motivation (or intrinsic interest in the subject) is seen as being the most desirable type of motivation to promote learning as it leads to 'deep learning' approaches and learning outcomes which are *concerned with conceptual understanding of the material, and incorporating this into one's existing knowledge*' (Fry, Ketteridge and Marshall, 2003: 65). However, it is generally acknowledged that learners who have strong extrinsically motivating factors will do what is necessary to pass the course, and that strategic learners may not always engage in deep learning. Although this may not be the most desirable type of motivation for the most 'holistic' learning to take place, in terms of passing the course it is a highly motivating factor. So if we consider our adult learners are on externally accredited programme, how do we develop a curriculum that is inclusive and provides the best opportunities and motivations for learning? It may be more appropriate to develop individual learning plans for these learners which include smart targets for learning (Specific, Measurable, Achievable, Relevant and Time bound). This means that it is important to consider the individuals needs, abilities, preferred way of learning, desired learning targets and preferred method of assessment within those available and recognized by the external awarding body. Individual learning plans of this nature are reviewed on a one-to-one basis with the tutor. This type of approach to the inclusive curriculum can be considered to be one of the best approaches for adult learning groups of this nature as it is an approach that responds to the individual needs of the learners. Is this approach to planning learning appropriate for those on programmes learning for pleasure? Yes, as it is still desirable to have some structure and planning for the learning that is to take place, and all of the above may still apply. It is still important for the adult learners to have a say in what they are to learn within a given time frame. It is also important to have some strategies for measuring the learning that has taken place, even on a programme attended primarily for pleasure.

Learners on programmes that combine workplace learning and formal sessions in the classroom, such as modern apprenticeships, are likely to access a vocational curriculum. This means that they are likely to spend the majority of their time in the workplace and attend formal learning on a part-time basis, perhaps once a week. They are likely to be part of externally accredited programmes of learning leading to vocational awards. The curriculum planned for this group of learners is likely to be intense, due to the nature of attendance, with curriculum content planned for delivery in a relatively short space of time. The learning for this group of learners in the formal college setting is likely to be focused upon developing the underpinning knowledge that reinforces practical skills. These skills are likely to be primarily developed in the practice setting alongside workshops in a formal learning setting. When planning an inclusive programme for these learners, balance is important in respect of the expected range of knowledge and skills to be developed in the formal classroom/workshop.

Lave's (1990) theory of situated learning is one which may be appropriate to consider when thinking about designing an inclusive curriculum for these learners. Lave theorizes that learning, as it normally occurs, is a function of the activity, context and culture in which it occurs – it is 'situated'.

This contrasts with most classroom learning which involves knowledge that is abstract and out of context. The principles of situated learning are based on the idea that social interaction is a critical component of situated learning and that knowledge needs to be presented in an authentic context. This means that, Lave is saying that, learning in context and in 'real' situations is the most desirable way of promoting inclusion in the learning process. When this occurs, Lave believes that learners then become part of a 'Community of Practice' which embodies certain beliefs and behaviours to be acquired and that as the new learner moves from the periphery of the community to its centre, he/she becomes more active or engaged within the culture and eventually assumes the role of 'expert'. Lave and Wenger (1990) call this the process of legitimate peripheral participation. The use of situated learning and communities of practice may benefit learners in a group. They make learning 'real' and 'meaningful' in order to support the development of practical vocational skills in the workplace. This is further supported by the use of subject specialists who are able to deliver the academic content of a programme such as this and link it effectively to work practice.

There are increasing numbers of HE students being taught in the FE environment; this has increased significantly with the more recent development of Foundation Degrees (FDs) in Arts (FDA) and Sciences (FDS), which are primarily designed to provide degrees which are vocationally oriented for learners. However, these degrees, though having significant work-related content and assessment, also require active reading and use of referencing in written work. For learners on FDs, this can be a particular challenge, and as tutors involved in teaching and supporting these learners a barrier to inclusion can be the sudden shift in emphasis that the students may feel when moving from programmes such as National Vocational Qualifications (NVQs). The challenge here for inclusive practice and curriculum access may be around providing appropriate academic study skills support for individual learners. This could mean providing sessions on Harvard Referencing or taking the time in sessions to discuss the meanings of new or unfamiliar words.

All students at various points will encounter problems with their learning, whether they are considered to have a learning difficulty or disability or not. However, there may be additional challenges for students with learning problems who may be accessing any of the above types of programmes. According to Tummons (2009: 101), *The social model of disability puts its focus not on an individual, and thereby on any physical or mental disability that the person might have, but on the society within which they live.* He goes on to say that *under the social model of disability, the emphasis is on changing the world around us so that we all can participate in it.*

In summary, in learning situations the emphasis is on adapting the environment and redesigning teaching and learning activities in order to promote access to learning for all learners. This opposes the view of seeing the learning difficulty as a barrier to learning itself. In reality, this may not always be easy, but a good practitioner will strive to provide equality of opportunity for all; this is discussed further in the next chapter.

Although this chapter is primarily focused upon curriculum development for inclusive practice, one should not ignore the implications for inclusive practice with regard to how learning progress is measured. Assessment of learning becomes especially important when learners are on a curriculum which is to lead to a recognized award/qualification. In these instances, the requirements of awarding bodies have to be considered and the implications for this in terms of inclusive practice are complex. The chapter "Theories and Principles for Planning and Enabling Learning and Assessment" will explore this area in detail, but it is worth mentioning here that a measure of success for the inclusive curriculum will always be how successful the learning of all the students on the programme has been.

Case Study

Shaheen is planning her curriculum delivery for a group of learners that she is taking over from another experienced tutor. The group she is taking over is an adult literacy basic skills group in a community setting. She is in year two of her teacher training programme and has some experience of delivering to groups of learners in the FE college environment. Shaheen has always taught Level-2 communication skills to large groups who have been assessed to be at Level 2 in their communication, reading and writing skills. In her planning, she rarely considers differentiated approaches to promote inclusive practice as she teaches a large number of students in a large lecture theatre using didactic teaching methods and Q&A as the main teaching and formative assessment activities. Summative assessment is via the completion of a standard portfolio of evidence and a national test, both of which are mapped to key skills standards. On meeting with the tutor she is taking the session over from, Shaheen finds that the style of teaching preparation she has been used to will not be appropriate for this group of learners as they are at vastly different levels of ability from entry Level 1 to Level 2. This means that to ensure inclusivity and to meet the wider needs of the learners, the learning and assessment resources will have to be thought through carefully on an individual basis. Developing the session plan for this group will be a far more detailed process as individual learner needs will have to be considered and detailed individual learning outcomes will have to be set. Individualized resources will have to be identified and individual approaches to assessment (methods and resources for measuring learning) will need to be considered.

Activity 5.3

Select two groups that you are currently working with that have differing profiles. Select a session plan you have devised for each group and evaluate their content in terms of promoting inclusive practice by answering the following questions. Can you identify where you have planned individual learning outcomes to meet the learners' needs? Can you identify where you have planned individualized approaches (strategies) to teaching and learning? Have you identified specific assessment strategies that are appropriate to the learners' needs and abilities and devised/located resources that are appropriate both for supporting learning and measuring learning (assessment) in a fair, equitable and accessible way?

Reviewing, evaluating and adapting curriculum to promote inclusive practice

Activity 5.4

Think about a group of learners that you have recently delivered a programme of learning to. Ask yourself the following questions:

- Do you feel you delivered a truly inclusive curriculum?
- If not, what issues were there with the curriculum delivery that you can identify, and how do you know that there were inclusion issues; in other words, on what evidence do you base this judgement on?
- List three things that you would change if you had the opportunity to deliver this curriculum again to promote fully inclusive practice?
- What constraints can you identify that may prevent you from implementing all the changes that you might wish?

Feedback

As a professional teacher, you will always be striving to improve your practice, and one of the ways that you can do this is by evaluation of and reflection on the programmes you have delivered in order to review how successful the delivery was and how any future deliveries of the programme can be improved.

Tummons (2009) provides some examples of trainee teachers' responses to the question, what is evaluation? – finding out if your course or curriculum did what it set out to do, judging fitness for purpose, seeing if the resources you use are at an appropriate standard, making sure the students get from the course what they expect to get, and what everyone else expected they would get.

This is a brief list, but it does provide a starting point to discuss the concept and process of evaluating curriculum delivery with regard to inclusive practices.

What are the best ways of gathering information about the success of the curriculum deliver? Questionnaires are often used to gather learner views in respect of this issue. There are, however, many issues surrounding getting valid information. One of these issues is phrased as 'questionnaire fatigue'. Questionnaires are used more and more by educational organisations, and students may appear to pay less and less attention to completing them, perhaps not realising that the information they provide is going to have an impact on future groups of students' experiences. Questionnaires may also be less than 'user friendly' as they can be difficult to understand and complete. A learner with poor reading skills may not be able to understand the questions, and a learner who is visually impaired may not be able to read the questions in the format they are presented in. In summary, questionnaires can be useful in providing some information about the success of the curriculum delivery, but as professional teachers we should be looking at complementary quantitative and qualitative ways of evaluating the curriculum so that we can improve the future experiences of our students.

A quantitative measure of the success of the programme may be represented by 'success' and 'refer' rates. If a programme has a high retention and completion rate than we may assume that all is well with the curriculum delivery. If, however, large numbers of students are leaving programmes before completion, or if students are being retained, yet the pass rate for the programme is very low, there may be issues with the way the curriculum has been designed and delivered. These complex issues may not be picked up by the process of a tick-box questionnaire.

In order to make an informed decision regarding future actions or changes to curriculum delivery, questionnaire data can be useful, but it is always important to give a detailed analysis of what is impacting upon learning and teaching experiences. One of the most effective ways of gathering information from students is by meeting with and talking to them. These meetings may be referred to as 'staff–student programme boards'. They can offer opportunities for staff and students to identify and discuss issues within programme and for the group collectively to identify where there are issues with programme design and delivery. These meetings can be vital in helping a programme team and programme tutor to plan for future improved delivery of the programme. The outcomes of meetings such as this will have formal future actions noted for those responsible for the future delivery of the curriculum.

Another way of evaluating the success or otherwise of the curriculum is by looking at the learning journey of learners. Have they achieved what they set out to do? If they have, why? Did you adapt your teaching strategies and the resources used to enable the learners to have full access to the curriculum? Did you provide alternative assessment methods? Did you ensure that students were provided with effective tutorial support as and when they needed it? Conversely, if you have learners who have not progressed as they would have wished, what are the reasons for this? Did you plan and deliver the curriculum in a way that is inclusive for the group of students? Did you consider them as individuals within a group at the session planning stage? Are the issues with progression to do with factors outside the curriculum delivery itself, such as poor attendance or personal problems that have impinged upon their learning? Have you failed to meet individual learner needs by not adapting your teaching approaches to support each learner's learning and progression?

In order to evaluate the progress of groups and individual learners and to plan for improved future practices, it can be useful to use a framework for reflection that will help you to focus upon key issues and what can be done to address them. A recognized model of reflective practice that can be particularly useful is Brookfield's (1985) notion of 'critical lenses'. According to Brookfield, there are four critical lenses for reflecting on practice. These 'lenses' are as follows:

Our own perspective
The point of view of our learners
The point of view of our colleagues
The point of view of established theory

Using Brookfield's critical lenses is a useful and practical framework that can be used by tutors in the Lifelong Learning Sector to evaluate information and produce an action plan for change based upon that information. Consider the following case study:

Case Study

Marcus is completing a review of his midyear learner questionnaire feedback as part of the process of reviewing a programme of study that he has delivered for the first time. Although generally the data is positive, there are one or two areas that have been raised that are of concern to Marcus. This first is that 25 per cent of the students have identified that the resources they were provided with were not useful in supporting the outcomes of the session, and second, 20 per cent of the students felt that the teaching and learning methods used were not useful to them. Marcus is aware that there is a forthcoming staff–student programme board, and he decides to try and find out from the students what the issues have been so that he can plan for and improve his future practice. At the programme board, Marcus is surprised by the feedback he receives. One student representative is one of the learners who gave negative comments about the two areas indicated. When he is asked if he is prepared to expand on the issues, the learner informs Marcus that he is happy to do so and informs Marcus that he has a specific learning difficulty with reading (dyslexia) and that on occasions the hand-outs that are provided are confusing. The learner also informs Marcus that he often delivers large amounts of content orally and that he cannot take in such large amounts of information as he has short-term memory problems and issues with processing and retaining information. Following the meeting, Marcus thinks about the issues that have been raised and decides to consult with his more experienced colleagues to see if they have any practical advice for him. At the same time, he decides that he needs to be more aware of the problems associated with the specific learning difficulty (dyslexia) and reads around the subject to increase his knowledge. Following these two activities, Marcus thinks that he is in a position to address the needs of this particular learner, and he arranges a tutorial to discuss what can be done for the remainder of the programme to support his individual needs. The outcome of this meeting is that Marcus will review the content of hand-outs to be provided to the learner. Marcus decides that the best way forward is to record his sessions and place them as a 'sound file' in the virtual learning environment, realising that this will benefit all the students in the class and not just the one learner. As Marcus is now more aware of the issues the learner faces, he is more conscious of the way he delivers the content of the sessions and he tries to build in different strategies for presenting information, such as visual aids. In going through this process, Marcus has inadvertently used Brookfield's critical lenses to reflect on and evaluate his own practice in order to make real changes to benefit teaching and learning.

Activity 5.5

Evaluate the process that Marcus has gone through in terms of Brookfield's critical lenses. When you are next provided with the opportunity to evaluate your practice, apply Brookfield's critical lenses as a tool for the reflective process.

Equality and diversity – Ethical and legal issues and curriculum development for inclusive practice

Activity 5.6

Locate your organization's Equal Opportunities Policy; this may be available from Human Resources and may also be available on your organization's website. Read it through and note how many references there are to legislation and how many different Acts of Law are mentioned.

Feedback

As a trainee teacher, it is important that you are aware of the legislation surrounding your profession and the implications for your teaching practice. It is also important to be aware of the legislation protecting your students. This section attempts to give a brief overview of some of the key areas of legislation you need to be aware of when designing curriculum development for inclusive practice. There is discussion of stereotyping of individuals, potential issues around gender balance, ethnicity and cultural issues.

The Disability Discrimination Act was passed in 1995, was extended in 2002 and amended in 2005. The original legislation was passed to protect disabled people from discrimination and defined disability as follows: *A person has a disability if he or she has a physical or mental impairment, which has a substantial and long-term adverse effect on his/her ability to carry out normal day-to-day activities.*

In 2001, the Special Educational Needs and Disability Act (2001), also known as SENDA (Part 4 of the DDA), brought education into the remit of the DDA. This extension, which was implemented in September 2002, ensured that FE colleges and the Local Authorities had legal responsibility not to treat disabled learners less favourably than others for reasons related to their disability as well as providing reasonable adjustments for disabled learners (2001). This Act uses a broader spectrum in defining disability as the legislation refers to *people with physical or sensory impairments, dyslexia, medical conditions, mental health difficulties and learning difficulties.*

The 2002 extension to the Act is particularly important for those in the teaching profession as it relates directly to educational organizations. This means that it is important for practitioners, FE colleges and the Local Authorities to *anticipate* the needs of learners rather than *respond* to the needs of learners as they might arise within the educational context.

As a result of this legislation, it is deemed as being desirable that educational organizations have in place the mechanisms to encourage disclosure of a disability. The ideal aim is for adjustments to be made prior to learners joining the programme. This may be done via the recruitment and interview process. Following the 2002 extension to the Act, many organizations offering educational programmes reviewed their recruitment and interview procedures. These reviews were completed in order to encourage applicants to disclose disabilities that could impact upon their educational progress prior to joining educational programmes. However, according to Tummons (2009: 100), it is important to bear in mind that *students are not obliged to tell anyone they have a disability* and that it *is possible for a student with a disability to feel that they have been discriminated against even if they have not revealed the disability.*

Tummons (2009) goes on to indicate that the legislation is there to provide a framework that should be liberating and not oppressive for teachers to work within and that at all times it is important not to lose sight of the concept of 'reasonableness' when adapting buildings or practice. Tummons (2009: 100) indicates some areas of practice where adjustments should be made, such as *adjustments to the exterior of buildings, to course materials, to assessment practices and to classrooms and workshops.* Tummons then goes on to stress that trainee teachers should not feel isolated when planning a curriculum to ensure inclusivity. This means that it is important to use all available support mechanisms, such as seeking specialist advice from learning difficulty and disability coordinators. Other sources of support may include practice mentors, other more experienced teachers, awarding bodies and external support networks such as action groups for the disabled. The learners themselves should always be at the centre of the process and where possible, guidance from them as to meeting their needs should be sought. Consider the following case study:

Case Study

Robert, a trainee teacher, has been approached by the college's coordinator for students with learning difficulties and/or disabilities. The coordinator informs Robert that a student, Sophie, who is visually impaired, has been accepted on the course he has become programme leader for and that in a meeting held with Sophie to establish her needs the following information was agreed. Sophie requires that handouts need to be enlarged by 20 per cent; Sophie needs to be at the front of the teaching room, and she has requested that a seat be kept near the front of the room for her. Sophie has also requested that, for as much time as possible, the tutor faces the front when delivering the content of the sessions to enable her to engage more fully with the teacher's delivery of the teaching content. It was also agreed that Sophie will be accompanied by a teaching assistant during teaching. This teaching assistant will take classroom notes and assist Sophie in the learning process in order to take care of her pastoral needs.

Robert is keen to support the student, but he is unsure about the practicalities of achieving this aim. Robert decides to meet with the student to discuss ways of improving the educational experience. Robert also plans to meet with his practice mentor, an experienced tutor, for assistance and guidance at regular intervals during his delivery of the programme. This is in order to discuss practical advice in ensuring that Sophie is fully included in the learning process. Robert is aware that meeting Sophie's needs will at times mean extra preparation work for him, but he is keen to support Sophie's progress as much as possible.

Activity 5.7

When you are planning the teaching for your next class, take time to consider where you have made 'reasonable adjustments' in your planning to accommodate the needs of your learners. How will this manifest itself in practice when you are delivering the session and what additional work, if any, does this lead to when preparing and delivering the session itself?

There are a range of additional issues to consider when thinking about equality and diversity and the inclusive curriculum. Some of these issues include the impressions of the learners and the teacher, the dangers of stereotyping, gender issues, cultural considerations and consideration of ethnicity.

In terms of curriculum development for inclusive practice, it is the teacher's job to remove as many barriers to learning as possible. According to Petty (2004), the first impressions formed from both the teachers' and learners' side can have a lasting influence on the development of any relationship as these first impressions can be difficult to overcome. Petty goes on to argue that when we meet a person for the first time, we subconsciously select information that we process in order to characterize a person. Petty (2004: 77) states that these characterizations are based upon factors such as *dress, hairstyle, facial expressions, posture, gestures, age, ethnic origins, gender as well as what the person says or how they say it.* This occurs so that we can best evaluate how to deal with or approach someone for the first time. Petty (2004: 79) defines stereotyping as *the tendency to attribute, to an individual, traits that we assume are characteristics of the group to which we believe they belong. This, of course, tends to blind the perceiver to the differences between the members of a group.*

As a tutor it is important to ensure that we design the curriculum to be inclusive but also that the learners feel that they are positively and equally valued when participating in the learning process. As trainee teachers, it is unlikely that you will set out to provide unequal opportunities for your learners, but according to Petty (2004) most teachers will do this. The argument runs that females get less class attention than males, less access to equipment such as computers and that tutors are often unaware of this. Petty also points out that learners from ethnic minorities and learners with learning difficulties and/or disabilities, shy learners or less able or disruptive learners may get unequal teaching in the classroom from some teachers. Moreover, the teachers are often unaware that this is happening.

It is highly unlikely that as a trainee teacher you will set out to be as inclusive as possible in your teaching, but it is essential to be aware of the possible 'pitfalls' in order to provide yourself with the best opportunity of avoiding them. As a teacher, you will need to be aware of some strategies that can help you to address potential inequality at a practical level. According to Gravells and Simpson (2009), there are a number of ways that you can do this throughout your teaching. Examples include taking the time to learn the names of your learners and using these names regularly to make each learner feel fully included in the learning process. It is also important to negotiate and set 'ground rules' for behaviour within the classroom, beginning with the use of appropriate ice-breakers to help to set the expected parameters for acceptable and unacceptable behaviour. This ought to facilitate a mutually respective learning environment. During the delivery of the teaching sessions, time should be taken to discuss issues such as equality and diversity policies and equality issues. If possible you should plan for additional tutorial support for those learners who require it. This can be established by using the entry data from the learners and also by engaging in individual discussions with learners. It is also important to ask the learners about their experiences at identified points in the programme, such as at the beginning, middle and end of the programme, to gauge their feeling about key issues in this area. As a trainee teacher, you also need to be aware that learners may stereotype you, and you should think carefully about the image you wish to project to your learners during the learning process.

Case Study

David is 35 years old and in his post-qualifying year a teacher. He may be considered to be unusual due to him being an 'early years' specialist, an area of teaching in which there are a minority of males. David is meeting his class of all female NVQ Level-3 students for the first time. David decides that for the initial session he will wear more formal dress to set the tone for the session and to create a professional impression. As his relationship develops with the students over the coming weeks, he may relax this dress code and begin to wear more casual clothing. Why do you think David has done this?

Activity 5.8

Think about the way you dress for teaching? Does your dress code change depending upon the subject you are teaching and the group of students you are working with? Select two groups from different programmes you teach upon? Evaluate why you chose to dress as you did.

Appraising the curriculum

A curriculum may be defined as a programme of learning undertaken by individuals and groups of learners. Who accesses these programmes and why is it dependent upon a range of complex issues. Some of these issues can include political agendas such as widening participation which has impacted heavily upon the types of learning programmes that are offered by FE colleges. Other factors may be regarded as being more localized, such as personal factors, social factors and economic factors, all or some of which may prevent an individual accessing a programme of learning. In order to promote inclusion in learning, it is important to be aware of potential barriers and have strategies in place to help potential learners to overcome them.

It may seem like a relatively routine process to plan a curriculum. A scheme of work is developed based upon the requirements of the curriculum. The reality may be different. The availability of resources, such as time, staffing and rooming/equipment, can all impact upon the curriculum. This means that designing an inclusive curriculum can be a complex process as the needs of individual learners have to be considered.

Inclusive practice is about differentiated practice, about providing the best possible opportunity for learning to take place for all learners, or matching what you teach to the individual learning needs of each learner in the group. This can be a very complex process, and even with the best of intentions it is not always possible to do this. This is because there may be financial constraints on you as a teacher in respect of the resources you can access. It may not be possible to secure the most appropriate teaching room to deliver your curriculum. You may need to adapt your teaching strategies to fit in with the resources that are made available to you. You may not always have time to prepare your resources exactly as you wish, and this means that you may need to be flexible in your style of teaching delivery. This may not be ideal, but a good teacher develops the ability to think on his or her feet and to adapt teaching and learning practice to make learning for all as accessible as possible.

There are lots of ways that you can gain information about how successful a curriculum delivery has been. As we have already seen, one important form of feedback comes from your students. Student feedback is important as this tells us how the curriculum has been received by the learners. This feedback and quantitative data, such as pass/fail rates, can provide a real and valuable basis for planning future curriculum change. We have also suggested that in order to review the curriculum it is useful to adopt some frameworks for reflection, such as Brookfield's (1985) critical lenses. This may enable you to review the curriculum by considering the learning experiences of yourself, your students, and your colleagues. Considering these experiences helps you to redesign the curriculum so that it can become more inclusive for the future.

We have also recommended that teachers in the Lifelong Learning Sector need to be aware of the key legislation surrounding the Disability Discrimination Act (2005). It is important to be aware of your organizational practices with regard to Equal Opportunities and the recruitment and selection of learners with regard to disclosure of learning difficulties and/or disabilities. Learners are not required to disclose a learning difficulty or disability, and this can cause a real dilemma for teachers; in other words, how can you plan a reasonable adjustment when you are not sure what the requirements are? The initial response to this question may be to plan your delivery to be as inclusive as possible. You will always be required to respond to the needs of your learners, and at times it is wise to take advice from more experienced practitioners if you are concerned about the progress of your learners. When thinking about other aspects of inclusion, stereotyping may be difficult to avoid on both the part of teachers and learners. You should try to avoid making 'snap' judgements, as far as you can, on your first impressions of any learner. This means that you need to give yourself time to get to know your learners in order to gain a better personal knowledge of them and their individual needs. This can include the aspirations of your learners. It may include cultural and religious beliefs.

This can help you to form a balanced judgement and should help you to plan for a truly inclusive curriculum for each learner. You also need to remember that the initial image of yourself that you project to your learners may leave them with a lasting impression, so you need to consider carefully the image you wish to project to your learners.

Summary of key points

Due to the nature of the Lifelong Learning Sector, there will always be pressures that influence the curriculum. It is important that we work as positively as possible within these constraints to prove as inclusive a learning experience by using all the available resources at our disposal. Inclusive practice is about meeting the diverse needs of all of the learners as far as possible. It is about using differentiated approaches in teaching and learning. This means that using a range of sources of information for reviewing and evaluating the curriculum is important so that you can reflect fully on the curriculum and plan for any future changes. There are legal frameworks that you have to work within as a teacher, and you need to be aware of these, especially in relation to anticipating learners' needs. Ignorance in respect of this matter is no defence! The consequence of this is that you need to be aware of wider issues for inclusion, such as the danger of stereotyping learners. It is also important that you have a sense of who you are and the image you want to project. Since first impressions often last with learners, they can set the foundation for future learning relationships.

This chapter links to the following SVUK Professional Standards:

Professional Values

AS1: All learners, their progress and development, their learning goals and aspirations and the experience they bring to their learning.
AS3: Equality, diversity and inclusion in relation to learners, the workforce and the community.
AS4: Reflection and evaluation of their own practice and their continuing professional development as teachers.
AS5: The importance of reflecting on and evaluating own practice as teachers, tutors or trainers against the value base of QTLS.
AS6: The application of agreed codes of practice and the maintenance of a safe environment.
AS7: Improving the quality of their practice.
DS1: Planning to promote equality, support diversity and to meet the aims and learning needs of learners.
DS2: Learner participation in the planning of learning.
FS2: Providing support for learners within the boundaries of the teacher role.
FS4: A multi-agency approach to supporting development and progression opportunities for learners.

⇨

Professional Knowledge and Understanding

AK3.1: Issues of equality, diversity and inclusion.

AK5.1: The impact of own practice on individuals and their learning.

AK6.1: Relevant statutory requirements and codes of practice.

AK6.2: Ways to apply relevant statutory requirements and the underpinning principles.

BK4.1: Good practice in meeting the needs of learners in collaboration with colleagues.

DK 1.1: How to plan appropriate, effective, coherent and inclusive learning programmes that promote equality and engage with diversity?

FK 1.1: Sources of information, advice guidance and support to which learners might be referred.

FK2.1: Boundaries of own role in supporting learners.

FK4.1: Professional specialist services available to learners and how to access them.

FK4.2: Processes for liaison with colleagues and other professionals to provide effective guidance and support for learners.

Professional Practice

AP 3.1: Apply principles to evaluate and develop own practice in promoting equality and inclusive learning and engaging with diversity.

AP5.1: Reflect on and demonstrate commitment to improvement of own teaching skills through regular evaluation and the use of feedback.

AP 6.1: Conform to statutory requirements and apply codes of practice.

AP 6.2: Demonstrate good practice through maintaining a learning environment which conforms to statutory requirements and promotes equality, including appropriate consideration of the needs of children, young people and vulnerable adults.

BP4.1: Collaborate with colleagues to encourage learner progress.

DP1.1: Plan coherent and inclusive learning programmes that meet learners' needs and curriculum requirements, promote equality and engage with diversity effectively.

FP1.1: Refer learners to information on potential current and future learning opportunities and appropriate specialist support services.

FP2.1: Provide effective learning support, within the boundaries of the teaching role.

FP4.1: Provide general and current information about a range of relevant external services.

FP4.2: Work with colleagues to provide guidance and support for learners.

Self-assessment questions

Question 1: How can you best define inclusive practice?

Question 2: What are some of the key planning considerations you need to make in the design of a truly inclusive curriculum? List them.

Question 3: Reflections on experiences of curriculum delivery are an important part of planning to improve future practice. Brookfield's critical lenses are one method of doing this. What are the four aspects of this process?

Moving on feature

This chapter has introduced you to curriculum development for inclusive practice. Try to think of how the material in this chapter can be applied to help you to design inclusive curricula within different educational contexts in order to meet the needs of a variety of learning groups.

Further reading

Clements, P. and Jones, J. (2005), *The Diversity Training Handbook: A Practical Guide to Understanding and Changing Attitudes*. London: Kogan Page.

Department for Education and Skills (2001), *Access for All*. London: DfES.

Kelly, A. V. (2004), *The Curriculum: Theory and Practice*. London: Age Publications.

Learning and Skills Council (2007), *Equality and Diversity – What's That Then?* East Midlands: LSC.

National Institute for Adult Continuing Education (2003), *New Rights to Learn: A Tutor Guide to Teaching Adults after the Disability Discrimination Act Part l*. Leicester: NIACE.

Neary, M. (2002), *Curriculum Studies in Post-Compulsory and Adult Education*. Cheltenham: Nelson Thornes.

Press for Change (2007), *Guidance on Trans-Equality in Post School Education*. London: Unison.

Preston, J. and Hammond, C. (2002), *The Wider Benefits of Further Education: Practitioner Views*. London: Centre for Research on the Wider Benefits of Learning.

Rogers, J. (2007), *Adults Learning* (5th edition). Buckingham: Open University Press.

Sanderson, A. (2001), 'Disabled students in transition: a tale of two sectors' failure to communicate'. *Journal of Further and Higher Education*, 25, (2) 227–240.

Thomas, L. (2001), *Widening Participation in Post-Compulsory Education*. London: Continuum.

Tummons, J. (2007), *Becoming a Professional Tutor in the Lifelong Learning Sector*. Exeter: Learning Matters.

White, L. and Weaver, S. (2007), *Curriculum for Diversity Guide*. Leicester: NIACE

References

Beck, R. C. (1990), *Motivation Theories and Principles* (3rd edition). New Jersey: Simon and Schuster.

Brookfield, S. (1985), *Becoming a Critically Reflective Teacher*. San Francisco: Jossey-Bass.

Brown, S., Armstrong, A. and Thompson, G. (1998), *Motivating Students*. Birmingham: SEDA Publications.

Coffield, F. (2004), *Learning Styles*. London: LSDA Publications.

Fry, H., Ketteridge, S. and Marshall, S. (2003), *A Handbook for Teaching and Learning in Higher Education* (2nd edition). London: Routledge Falmer.

Gardner, H. (1993), *Frames of Mind: The Theory of Multiple Intelligences* (2nd edition). London: Fontana Press.

Gravells, A. and Simpson, S. (2009), *Equality and Diversity in the Lifelong Learning Sector*. Exeter: Learning Matters.

Kelly A. V. (1999), *The Curriculum, Theory and Practice* (4th edition). London: Paul Chapman.

Kennedy, H. (1997), *Learning Works*. London: Further Education Funding Council.

Knowles, M. (1984), *Andragogy in action*. San Francisco: Jossey Bass.

Lave, J. and Wenger, E. (1990), *Situated Learning: Legitimate Peripheral Participation*. Cambridge: Cambridge University Press.

McDonald, J. & Lucas, N. (2000), The impact of FEFC funding 1997-1999: research on 14 colleges. *Journal of Further and Higher Education*, 32, (3) 373–384.

Petty, G. (2004), *Teaching Today* (3rd edition). Cheltenham: Nelson Thornes.

Tennant, M. (1997), *Psychology and Adult Education* (2nd edition). Oxfordshire: Routledge.

Tomlinson, C. A. (1997), *Differentiation of Instruction in Mixed Ability Classrooms*. Idaho: Idaho Council for Exceptional Children.

Tomlinson, C. A. (2001), *How to Differentiate Instruction in Mixed Ability Classrooms* (2nd edition). Alexandria: Association for Supervision and Curriculum Development.

The Tomlinson Report (1996), London: Stationery Office.

Tummons, J. (2009), *Curriculum Studies in the Lifelong Learning Sector*. Exeter: Learning Matters.

Vygotsky, L. S. (1978), *Mind in Society, The Development of Higher Psychological Processes*. Cambridge, MA: Harvard University Press.

Websites

Andragogy (M. Knowles) Theory into Practice, http://tip.psychology.org/knowles.html

The Alexander Kapp. www.andragogy.net

Department for Education and Skills Disability Discrimination Act, http://nationalstrategies.standards.dcsf.gov.uk/node/84546 Disability Discrimination Act

Oxford English Dictionary On-line, http://www.oed.com/

Research Methods for the Lifelong Learning Sector 6

> **Learning Outcomes**
>
> After reading this chapter, you should be able to
>
> identify what the term 'research' means within the context of the Lifelong Learning Sector,
>
> analyse some of the ways that the research process can be used by practitioners within the Lifelong Learning Sector,
>
> critically appraise some of the ways that the research process can be applied to the Lifelong Learning Sector.

The chapter develops your knowledge and understanding of select research processes that inform the Lifelong Learning Sector. Through applying research to the Lifelong Learning Sector, it is possible to ensure that professional practice is as innovative as possible. This is because researching professional roles enables you to deepen your understanding of what is meant by the term 'best practice' within this area of education.

Introduction

This chapter explores key aspects of the research process. The content identifies a number of key research models, the methods that can be applied within the research process and aspects of good practice that are especially important if effective research is to happen. The research process is outlined, analysed and critically appraised in order to investigate how research methods can be applied to Lifelong Learning. As with previous chapters, there are formative activities that reinforce learning in relation to the main aspects of the research process.

Defining research

> **Activity 6.1**
>
> What is your understanding of the word research?
>
> **Feedback**
>
> Research is an important part of every academic discipline. The term means discovering new information about a subject. When we discover this new information, it enables us to confirm or dispute whether previous understandings of academic matters still apply. For example, if we are to apply 'learning preferences' to teaching within the Lifelong Learning Sector, it would appear to be preferable to base this decision on appropriate research findings.
>
> ⇨

We can say that there are two especially influential theories that have influenced the research process. These are the 'normative' and 'interpretive' models of research. The two theoretical perspectives provide opposing models of research. The normative perspective is scientific in its approach. This is because it recommends that the best way to gather research data is to adopt a scientific perspective in order to gather statistics and quantifiable data. In contrast, the interpretive perspective is non-scientific in its approach. Interpretive research attempts to gather the views and opinions of individuals in a non-statistical way. These narrative accounts are used to present individual interpretations of the social world. Both approaches to research are summarized in the following dictionary definition of research: *Diligent and systematic inquiry or investigation into a subject in order to revise facts, theories, applications* (Online dictionary).

Research is important for the Lifelong Learning Sector because it provides the opportunity to revise and reinforce understandings of this educational context. This means that being aware of the research process enables you to increase your knowledge of the latest findings about the factors influencing the learning process.

The research process

The research process is characterized by competing models of research. The previous section of the chapter refers to the normative and interpretive models of research. Both of these approaches have a distinctive philosophy of the research process. This means that the data-gathering methods that are chosen are influenced by the underlying research philosophy. Whereas the normative approach to research emphasizes the importance of 'scientific processes', the interpretive perspective is non-scientific in its outlook. This results in data-gathering methods that are concerned with gathering non-scientific or qualitative data.

Competing perspectives

As well as the normative and interpretive research perspectives, 'action research' is another influential research perspective. This research model emphasizes the importance of researching professional practice so that the findings can be used to influence future work. This approach to research is often used within education so that the findings can be applied to improve professional practice. In the previous section, we exemplified 'learning preferences' as an educational initiative for the Lifelong Learning Sector. A potentially interesting action research project might be an analysis of the success or otherwise of the application of learning preferences within the Lifelong Learning Sector. These various research perspectives are described as being in competition because they can have a conflicting understanding of the research process and how this process should be applied.

Research methods

Research methods refer to the data-collection processes that are applied by researchers. The data that are gathered are in general either 'quantitative' (or statistical) or 'qualitative' (or non-statistical). The research methods employed by the researcher are either 'primary' (or the immediate work of the researcher) or 'secondary' (in other words, using the findings of other published researchers). The techniques used to gather these data can include questionnaires, interviews, observations, focus groups, case studies and book-based research in 'learning resource centres'.

Validity

Validity refers to the acceptability of the research. There are accepted conventions followed by academic researchers, for example, being aware of ethical issues. This means that it is important for researchers to be able to identify what is accepted as being 'good practice' within research. Research should not be used to harm others. There should always be consent and openness within any research project. If these principles are not apparent, this can mean that the research is not valid or acceptable. To accurately assess whether to apply 'learning preferences' to the Lifelong Learning Sector, it is important to ensure that this particular research question has been answered appropriately by following acceptable research conventions.

Four types of validity are 'face validity', 'content validity', 'empirical validity' and 'predictive validity'.

Face validity

This aspect of validity asks whether the research methods within a research project measure what should be measured. For example, are the data that are gathered by an initial questionnaire used to generate semi-structured interviews or are the two processes unrelated? If the research methods are unrelated to each other, the validity or acceptability of the research can be questioned. If you were doing a research project on 'learning preferences' you might generate data with an initial questionnaire and then support these data with a series of semi-structured interviews.

Content validity

Content validity relates to the theoretical content of the research process. Have key concepts been covered by the research? If they have, this means that the research is more likely to be valid. Research projects often have a 'literature review' section. This is one way of attempting to show that key concepts have been covered. In assessing the viability of 'learning preferences', it is important to consider other academic analyses of this topic. This consideration is likely to complement your own research data.

Empirical validity

This element of validity asks whether the research data support the research question in a broad way. Do the data that have been gathered answer the research question in enough depth and detail? Have sufficient data been gathered or is there a need for more data gathering if the research question is to be answered comprehensively? A disadvantage of a 'small-scale' research project on 'learning preferences' is that the data are 'localized' to the project. It is not possible to make generalizations, and this lessens the empirical validity of the research.

Predictive validity

This aspect of validity looks at whether accurate predictions for the future can be made as a result of the research. Have definite findings been obtained that give enough depth and substance to predict future developments for the research area? The ideal for educational research is that the findings can be used to inform future practice. This is only possible if the predictive value of the research is robust.

Reliability

'Reliability' refers to the accuracy or otherwise of the research findings. The ideal is for the research to produce consistent findings. If the research is characterized by this consistency of findings over time, this adds to the quality of the research process. Like validity, there are a number of different types of reliability within research.

Inter-observer reliability

This example of reliability refers to different researchers finding similar research findings. The discovery of this 'pattern' means that the research process has identified consistent findings.

Test–retest reliability

This form of reliability uses the same methodology to produce consistent findings on a number of occasions. Once more, it is the discovery of a 'pattern' within the research that means we can say that the research is reliable.

Inter-item reliability

This type of reliability means that different research methods are used in order to produce consistent findings. As an example, questionnaire data may be used to inform a semi-structured interview and a focus group. If the findings from these research methods are consistent, this will add to the reliability of the research findings.

Triangulation

This term has been popularized by Norman Denzin and Lincoln (2000). Triangulation means that the researcher uses a number of ways of gathering research data. As an example, a researcher might use questionnaires, interviews and library research as the three sources of data. As long as the data have been gathered effectively and there is depth and detail of content, the subsequent theory is more likely to be valid and reliable. Like 'reliability' and 'validity', there are different ways of showing that you have triangulation of data.

Methodological triangulation

This type of triangulation is characterized by the researcher using many different but complementary research methods within a research project.

Data triangulation

This form of triangulation draws on many different but complementary sets of data within the same research project.

Investigator triangulation

This form of triangulation uses the research findings of many different researchers to inform the same research project.

Theory triangulation

This type of triangulation uses a number of different but relevant theories to interpret the research findings within a research project.

Research ethics

Researchers need to be aware of ethical good practice. Ethics refers to applying moral principles in order to ensure that the research subjects are never harmed by the research process. Opie (2004: 25) defines research ethics as 'the application of moral principles to prevent harming or wronging others, to promote the good, to be respectful and fair'. It may be possible to find out what your learners really think of learning preferences by attaching hidden microphones to the classroom desks and recording everything they say during an activity that is based on learning preferences. The difficulty with his course of action is that it goes against the principles of 'informed consent' and the research process becomes unethical. This means that ethics needs to be considered at all points of the study, from the design of the research question to interpreting the results and presenting the findings.

Designing the research question

It is important to ask yourself what you want to know and why you want to research into your chosen topic. This is so that you can confirm that you have a justifiable interest in your area of research. If your research is in any way 'experimental', it is important to consider the implications for those involved. Opie (2004: 25–6) emphasizes the importance of asking yourself about the 'potential consequences' of the research.

Procedures for data collection

When you are gathering research data, it is important to ensure that you never ask your research participants anything that you would not want to be asked. It is also important to make sure that you never ask people to do anything that you would not want to be asked to do. Opie (2004: 27) considers that these two points are 'the acid test' of good practice within research.

Research relationships

It is important to remember that you have a moral responsibility to the people that you are working with. Make sure that you do not manipulate the research relationship to get 'good data'. It is also important to be aware of the power relationship that exists between you and the research subjects. Opie (2004: 29) draws attention to the powerful position that you can be in as a researcher and the powerless position that may be experienced by those being 'researched'.

Data interpretation and analysis

It is important to be aware of any theoretical frameworks or value systems that might influence your data interpretation and analysis. The research process can be complicated, and it is important to acknowledge challenges in answering research questions as opposed to making the process appear 'neat' and 'uncomplicated'. Opie (2004: 30–1) emphasizes that protecting research subjects in written accounts is especially important if ethical principles are to be maintained.

Data dissemination

When you present your research findings, it is important to ensure that your research participants' anonymity is protected. The most essential principle is for you to avoid harming anyone during the research process. Opie (2004: 32) recommends that researchers always have to consider whether 'the ends justify the means' during the research process.

The Table 6.1 summarizes the essential points of good practice that need to be remembered if good practice within research is to be maintained:

Table 6.1 'Remember' research ethics

Remain true to your data in order to maintain professional integrity.

Ensure the physical, social, psychological well-being of research participants is never adversely affected.

Make your research participants know how far they will be given anonymity and confidentiality.

Excessive covert or 'hidden' research violates the principles of informed consent.

Make no threats to confidentiality and anonymity of research data.

Be especially careful if your research subjects are vulnerable because of age, disability, physical and/or mental health.

Extra care is required if your research involves children. The consent of parent and child must be sought.

Research participants need to know that they have the right to refuse to participate.

From this initial discussion about the research process, we can now explore the concept 'methodology'.

Activity 6.2

What do you think the word 'methodology' means?

Feedback

The word 'methodology' sounds like the word 'method'. A way of explaining this word is to think about studying different ways of doing research. There are different research methods or ways of completing research. We have previously identified the difference between the 'normative' and 'interpretive' approaches to doing research. Whereas the normative approach places an emphasis on 'scientific' methods, the interpretive approach is 'non-scientific' in its emphasis. 'Methodology' is a word that means the study of methods of data collection. It is important to emphasize that as well as differing theoretical approaches to gathering data, there are a number of different research methods. These research methods gather quantitative (numerical) and/or qualitative (non-numerical) data. The sort of data that are gathered depends on the approach of the researcher. If you have a scientific approach to your research question, you are likely to gather quantitative data. If you are non-scientific in your research approach you are likely to gather qualitative data. The methods that are used can include questionnaires, surveys, interviews, observation, focus groups, experiments and library research. These research methods can be used in isolation or combined together to produce comprehensive research findings. The number of methods being used depends upon the nature of the research question and the specific research objectives.

We can now add more detail to our discussion of research perspectives and data-collection methods. This is a way of setting the scene before we look at how the research process can be applied to the Lifelong Learning Sector.

The research models

In Table 6.2, there is a summary of three influential models of research with a brief description of their key features.

Table 6.2 Research models

Research model	Key features
Normative	This perspective was popularized initially by David Hume in the eighteenth century. It emphasizes the importance of 'scientific' approaches to understanding the world. This model of research is seen today in OFSTED inspection reports
Interpretive	This school of thought has been popularized by Edmund Husserl. It emphasizes the importance of non-scientific approaches to the research process. This model of research is seen today in research accounts that encourage teachers to become 'reflective practitioners'
Action research	This model of research has been popularized by Kurt Lewin since the 1940s. It emphasizes the importance of researching professional practice. The objective of the research is to improve future professional practice. The previous example about research assessing the effectiveness of 'learning preferences' is an example of action research

These models of research are especially useful to you as work within the Lifelong Learning Sector because of the influence they have had in shaping the research process. As a teacher, you will need to influence practitioners by drawing attention to examples of good professional practice. Knowledge and awareness of research about Lifelong Learning will help your professional development. As with the psychological perspectives we considered in Chapter 4, the origins of the ideas in these models of research go back to some of the important philosophical ideas that have influenced Western thought. Bryman (2004: 11) considers that the emphasis that is placed upon scientific practice within the normative perspective goes back to the ideas of the Enlightenment. This idea is central to the normative model of research so it can be claimed that the perspective has its intellectual origins in this classical thought. The interpretivist research paradigm emphasizes the importance of individuals establishing creative meaning with the social world. Bryman (2004: 13) equates this approach to research with 'phenomenology'. This in turn links the perspective to the ideas within humanism and interactionism. In other words, the genesis of the perspective's dominant idea can be linked to these theoretical perspectives. A summary of each of the three research perspectives follows. A definition of each of the key perspectives is given, key figures influencing the perspective are identified and central terms within each perspective are explained.

Normative research

The normative model of research is based on scientific principles. David Hume is associated with this perspective. This research model tends to be grounded in measurable or 'statistical' data. This means that the perspective is based on precise measurements that test theoretical perspectives by applying reason to identify whether the theory can be proven. Research that is based on this perspective usually begins with a hypothesis proposing a correlation or relationship. The objective of the subsequent research process is to identify whether the hypothesis is correct. This then enables the researcher to produce broad generalizations that allow scientific theory to be generated.

Applying normative research to the Lifelong Learning Sector

Normative research is often used to reveal what is happening in the lives of children and families in the United Kingdom. There are numerous examples of where statistics are used to either prove or disprove an argument. An especially significant application of statistics to the Lifelong Learning Sector appears with OFSTED. The data used for inspections of Lifelong Learning establishments are often presented in a statistical format. These findings are quantified 'scientifically' in order to provide data about performance. A frequent strategy within this normative approach is to present statistical findings in combinations so that sets of statistics appear to be reinforcing other sets of data. In the above example, other statistics are used to support the inspection process. Statistical data about a particular educational institution is compared and contrasted to other similar institutions. These statistics are then used to present a 'definite' impression of educational performance. In other words, the statistics are used to present a large-scale general answer to question.

Interpretive research

Interpretivist research places an emphasis upon the importance of interpreting human experience. The perspective has been popularized by Edmund Husserl. In many respects the perspective is opposed to the normative model of research. Instead of emphasizing the importance of 'scientific analysis', 'hypotheses' and 'surveys', interpretive research focuses on individuals and how they experience the social world. This means that data gathering is regarded as reflecting the researcher's personal engagement with the research process. The process becomes as important as the data that have been gathered as there is the acknowledgement of the creativity of both the researcher and the research subjects. The consequence of this approach is that research becomes more narrative and less statistical.

Applying interpretive research to the Lifelong Learning Sector

In his book *Local Knowledge* (1993), Clifford Geertz argues that 'largeness of mind' comes from reflecting on how we interact with others. This process of reflecting on interaction is at the centre of the interpretivist approach to methodology. It can be argued that some of the most profound reflections of teaching have come from the interpretive model of doing research. This is revealed in Reece and Walker's (2007) text that draws on reflections of 'teaching, training and learning' to provide a comprehensive reflection on post-compulsory teacher education. The book is grounded in reflective practice, so it is particularly useful for those who are new to teaching. The interpretive approach to education is also exemplified by Lieberman's (2009) article about 'communities of professional practice'. Lieberman reflects on the importance of 'learning communities' for teaching by considering the contribution that 'reflective practice' can make to teaching and learning. This reflective practice is based on an interpretive paradigm that places a premium on using experience to inform future teaching. The implication of this interpretive approach is that a statistical focus may not account for the rich variety of experience within the educational context. It can be suggested that this is a particularly important benefit of the interpretive approach to research. The creativity of learners and their teachers may be more likely to be captured by placing an emphasis on researching the process of interaction. Lieberman (2009) develops Wenger's (1998) idea of 'communities of practice'. The idea runs that in a community of practice it is possible not only to 'see professional practice' but also to 'see through this practice' so that future teaching can develop accordingly. The interpretive model of research is a paradigm that is highly support-ive of this idea as it is based on the consideration of non-statistical processes.

Action research

This research perspective has been popularized by Kurt Lewin. The central purpose of action research is to improve professional practice through researching aspects of 'best practice'. Action research is developmental because the central aim of the research is to investigate practice with a view to developing professional roles. This means that action research does not attempt to discover general findings. It is research that is characterized by findings that are 'particular' and 'specific'. Action research is one of the most important forms of profes-sional research. It is a research process that has been described as being 'cyclical' and not linear. This is because the research process involves data gathering, reviewing the data that have been collected, planning for new action and in turn implementing new action.

Applying action research to the Lifelong Learning Sector

Action Research can be applied to the Lifelong Learning Sector by reflecting on professional practice. If there are elements of practice that are not working, it is possible to research what needs to be done to make improvements to this situation. It is also possible to identify the aspects of professional practice that are working well in order to inform future professional work. As the Lifelong Learning context is an area of education that can be characterized by innovative government policy initiatives, it appears to be constantly adapting to the latest interpretation of 'best practice'. This means that it is important to have action researchers who can inform and influence future policy initiatives. Examples of 'improvements' to educational practice for the Lifelong Learning Sector that have been recommended include becoming aware of the applications of 'brain gym', 'emotional intelligence', and 'learning preferences'. It can be argued that it is through action research that we are more likely to accurately assess the benefits of these educational initiatives. This is one of the reasons why there is so much interest in the action research paradigm.

Activity 6.3

Which of these research approaches do you think is the best approach to adopt as a researcher?

Feedback

The answer to this question is that the approach that is adopted depends upon the nature of your research question. If you are doing research on the number of learners who have improved their communication skills, it may be more appropriate to adopt a normative approach in order to gather statistics so that a 'large-scale' analysis can be completed. This is not to say that this research question could not be answered by a smaller scale focus that looks at the experiences of a few research participants. The approach that is adopted depends upon what the researcher wants to answer and how they want to respond to the research question. It may be that a combination of methods is used so that, as well as gathering statistics, there are also reflective accounts that are interpretive. In other words, the different research models are not necessarily opposed to one another. They can be used together to produce a comprehensive answer to the research question.

The research methods

Research methods gather data that are either qualitative (non-statistical) or quantitative (statistical) or a combination of both. If you are doing research, a range of methods are available to you. The methods that you will use for your research depend upon the nature of the research question you want to answer. If you have a small-scale area of focus, you are likely to use fewer data-collection methods. This may mean that you are inclined to use interpretive methods for gathering your data because you do not want to provide broad generalizations from your research. In other words, the research perspective that is adopted and the methods that are used are entirely driven by the research question and its associated objectives.

In general, the normative approach is considered to be a structured scientific approach. This means that a deductive approach is adopted that tests a specific hypothesis. The research process is concerned with exploring the relationships that exist between particular variables. If one adopts this research perspective, it is likely that the methods that are chosen are those that can gather large amounts of statistical data that can be quantified and used as a basis for broad conclusions.

In contrast, the research methods that are used within the interpretive perspective are relatively unstructured. The research is more likely to be 'inductive' or open ended in nature. The research methods are concerned with identifying the meaning of social interaction. These 'negotiated meanings' are used to establish theories that attempt to explain social interaction.

Example research methods

A number of research methods are available to researchers. The previous section has identified that the type of methods that are used for data gathering depend on the nature of the research question. Some of the popular data-gathering techniques are discussed in the following section.

Experiments
This type of data-collection method is used within the normative model of research. Experiments adopt a 'cause and effect' approach by seeking to prove or disprove a hypothesis.

Surveys
Surveys are used in order to 'pool' or obtain information about attitudes, beliefs and behaviours. Surveys are usually large scaled and they tend to be associated with the normative perspective and its attempt to answer a research question in a 'scientific' manner. Much of the data that are presented within OFSTED reports is based on statistical data about educational performance. This means that the reports are akin to 'surveys'.

Focus groups
Kreuger (1994) defines focus groups as being small structured groups (between four and 12 people) that are facilitated by the researcher. The aim of the focus group is to generate detailed discussion about an issue of relevance to the research question. These data are gathered via a semi-structured question-and-answer discussion. Kreuger (1994) emphasizes the importance of providing a permissive and non-threatening environment in order to generate detailed data. OFSTED often use focus-group data to complement their statistical data. During the inspection process, groups of learners are often asked to enter into a focus-group process in order to help the inspectors gather qualitative data about learning and teaching.

Interviews

Gillham (2000) defines an interview as a conversation between two people in which the interviewer seeks particular responses from the interviewee. There are different types of interview. There are structured interviews that are rigidly structured, with a set of questions that all the interviewees are expected to answer. There are semi-structured interviews where a series of prompts are used with the interviewees in order to facilitate more flexible discussion about particular issues. There are also unstructured interviews where the discussion is about an area of focus with no prior prompts provided by the interviewer.

Observation

As well as there being different sorts of interviews, there are also different forms of observation. We can distinguish between 'participant' and 'structured' observation. Structured observation is defined as being a quantitative analysis of actions, whereas participant observation is regarded as being a qualitative engagement in interaction. In other words, the type of observation that is done will link to the research paradigm that is being adopted by the researcher. OFSTED has completed observations of teaching that are based on 'structured' appraisals of teaching and learning that assess 'excellent', 'good', 'satisfactory' or 'unsatisfactory' performance.

Activity 6.4

What are the advantages and disadvantages of questionnaires and interviews?

Feedback

All of the above research methods have advantages and disadvantages. The methods that are used depend upon the research question that has been selected and the research objectives.

Questionnaires have the advantage of being able to gather quantitative and qualitative data. This is possible if you have a combination of closed and open questions. The 'yes/no' closed questions can be used to produce statistical data. The 'open' questions that request the views and opinions of research subjects can be used to gather qualitative data. Another advantage of questionnaires is that they can be issued to a large number of research subjects. If the questionnaire is well designed, this can mean that a large amount of data is gathered relatively quickly. Many students doing research find that a questionnaire is a useful way of beginning a research study. There is the possibility of gathering much initial data about the chosen area of study.

A disadvantage of questionnaires is that the questions can be misinterpreted by the research subjects. This means that it is important to ensure that the questions are written in a clear and unambiguous way. It is also important to ensure that the questions are organized in a logical way so that the research subjects can understand the rationale behind the questionnaire's design.

Interviews have the advantage of providing potentially 'rich' and detailed information about the research topic. If a researcher is interviewing a research subject for half an hour, there is the possibility of gathering much data. It is also possible to treat the interviewee as an 'individual', so their views and opinions are respected during the research process.

⇨

A disadvantage of interviews is that they are potentially time consuming. This means that you are unlikely to gather a large number of respondent views in a typical interview schedule. This in turn means that the research becomes small scale and localized. It may then be impossible to establish a general theory that can be applied on a broad scale. Another potential disadvantage of the interview process is the influence of the interviewer on the interviewee. The interviewee may give answers to 'please' the interviewer as opposed to really saying what they think about particular issues.

Analysing data

We have previously identified that there are quantitative (or statistical) and qualitative (non-statistical) sets of data. Once the data have been gathered, it needs to be analysed. This section of the chapter outlines some of the important aspects of the data analysing process.

Two example strands of data processing include 'quantitative data analysis' and 'qualitative data analysis'. Within quantitative data analysis, we can distinguish between 'descriptive' and 'inferential' statistics. Whereas descriptive statistics identify the nature of the data findings, inferential statistics are used to generate theory from statistical data. Within qualitative data analysis, we can use what is referred to as 'theme analysis' to generate theory from the qualitative data.

Descriptive statistics

Descriptive statistics are used to describe the numerical data that has been gathered. It makes sense that the first step in any statistical analysis is to describe the data that has been obtained. There are different types of descriptive statistics, and these include frequency distributions, measures of central tendency and measures of dispersion.

Frequency distributions

These descriptive statistics are used to describe the frequency of particular categories within a data set. This is exemplified in Table 6.3:

Table 6.3 Frequency distributions

Social class	Frequency	Percentage
1	7	17.5
2	15	37.5
3	8	20
4	6	15
5	4	10
Total	**40**	**100**

Measures of central tendency

These descriptive statistics provide a single figure to represent a data set as effectively as possible. Three popular ways of doing this are by presenting a 'mode', a 'median' and a 'mean'. The mode represents the most frequently occurring statistic, the median is the middle score in the data set and the mean is the arithmetic average score within a data set.

Measures of dispersion

Numerical data sets have differing degrees of internal variability. This means that each set of numerical data can differ according to the range that has been obtained. The 'range' in this instance refers to the highest and lowest scores within a set of data. An important term within this category of statistical analysis is 'standard deviation'. This term can be used to indicate how close or otherwise the statistical findings are to the average value. If you report that '68 per cent of all measurements fall within 1 standard deviation of the average', this indicates how close the data set is to the average value that has been obtained. In other words, if the average was '9', this would mean that 68% of the findings are between 7 and 10.

Levels of measurement

Within statistical data sets, there are four different levels of measurement that are used to interpret the information that has been gathered. These levels of measurement are referred to as 'nominal, ordinal, interval and ratio' measurements.

Nominal measurement

This term refers to measurements that are arranged according to categories. An example of nominal measurement can be seen with the following example of social class and its division into upper class, upper middle class, middle class, lower middle class, upper working class and lower working class.

Ordinal measurement

Ordinal measurement allows the data to be arranged in a numbered series. An example of ordinal measurement occurs if the respondents' attitudes are measured, with '1' representing 'most popular', '2' representing 'neutral' and '3' representing 'least popular'.

Interval measurement

This form of measurement has equal intervals between the points on the measurement scale. If you use whole numbers to present your statistical data, you are using interval measurement as the basis of your theoretical conclusions. An example of this type of measurement is temperature where the range might be from –20 to 30 degrees centigrade. If you were researching how climate differences influence types of teaching and learning activities on a global scale, you might use interval measurement to present your findings.

Ratio measurement

This type of measurement is similar to interval measurement, but it takes into consideration the intervals on the measurement scale in relation to 'absolute zero'. An example of ratio measurement can be seen with test scores where they are understood in relation to a score between 0 and 100.

Level of measurement and graphs

The type of measurement that is chosen in turn influences how the data should be presented. This is outlined in Table 6.4:

Table 6.4 Type of measurement and choice of graph

Type of measurement	Pie chart	Bar chart	Scattergram
Nominal	*	*	
Ordinal	*	*	*
Interval			*
Ratio			*

Pie Charts, Bar Charts and Scattergrams

Using charts to present your findings can be an effective way of presenting the data that you have obtained. The subsequent section gives three examples of a pie chart, a bar chart and a scattergram.

Example pie chart

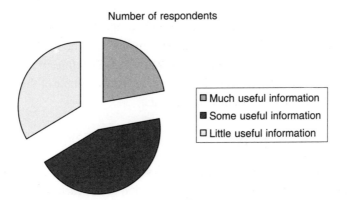

Number of respondents

☐ Much useful information
■ Some useful information
☐ Little useful information

Example bar chart

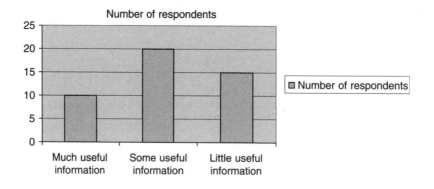

Example scattergram

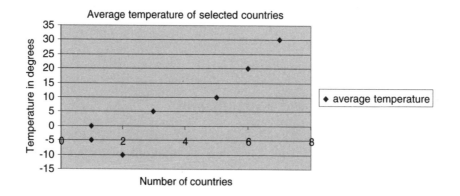

Inferential statistics

These statistics differ from descriptive statistics because they are used to generate theory as opposed to report findings. Inferential statistics look for the differences and the relationships between sets of data. These differences and relationships are then used to generate interpretations of the data. Alan Bryman and Cramer (1997: 4–5) defines inferential statistics as enabling the researcher to demonstrate that the results from a sample of the data set are likely to be found in any other random sample of the data.

Qualitative data analysis

The first stage in analysing qualitative data is to describe the data. You might want to present the main research findings and then write a paragraph about each of these main findings.

By doing this, you will be developing what Geertz (1973) refers to as 'thick description'. This means that you are developing thorough and comprehensive descriptions of the phenomena that are being studied. This 'thick description' gets its label from the depth of detail that is included about context, intentions, meanings and process.

Once the data has been described, it is possible to classify your findings or, in other words break ·the data down and put it back together in a meaningful way. This might mean that you have to develop 'categories' or 'headings' in order to organize and classify your data. Categorizing or classifying data enables you to 'funnel' your findings so that concepts can be compared and contrasted. This then enables you to look for patterns in the data that can be used to inform your theory. It provides you with the opportunity to explore the links that exist between categories. This in turn allows you to develop explanations that can explain these associations. Once you have analysed your qualitative data in this way, you can then develop theory from your data.

Activity 6.5

Think about each of the stages of the research process and suggest how you might investigate attitudes to 'healthy eating' within a FE College.

Feedback

One of the most important parts of the research process is to choose a manageable research focus. You can do this through thinking carefully about the title of your research. In the above example, it is important to show that you are not going to embark on a research project that is too big and unmanageable. If you have a title like 'Critical Appraisal of Attitudes Towards Healthy Eating in a Local FE College', you have a manageable focus for your research because you are doing your research on one organization. It is also important to ensure that your research objectives are manageable and that they show that you are aware of the importance of 'identifying, analysing and critically assessing' relevant issues. Never have too many objectives as it is hard to show that all the objectives have been achieved. In the above example research question, you might have the following three research objectives:

- identify attitudes to healthy eating in a local FE College,
- analyse attitudes to healthy eating in a local FE College,
- critically assess recent policy developments in view of the research findings.

Before beginning the research, you need to think about the research paradigm that will be applied to your study. In the above example question, all three of the research paradigms that we have referred to in the chapter are relevant to the question. This is because it is possible to gather statistics about healthy eating, so the normative model of research is relevant. In identifying 'attitudes', the interpretive paradigm is being applied. If the research findings are being used to make recommendations about how practice can be improved in the future, we can also say that the research question links to 'action research'.

Once you have identified your research paradigm, you need to think about how you will gather your data. The above research question can be answered through applying a combination of quantitative and qualitative data. You could design a questionnaire that has both closed and open questions in

⇨

order to gather statistical and non-statistical data. The closed questions, with their 'yes/no' responses, can be quantified. If you have a question like 'have you worked in the College for less than 5 years?' you can give a descriptive statistic that summarizes this finding within your research report. If you include an open question such as 'what are your views on healthy eating?' you can in turn gather the attitudes and views of your respondents. In order to show that you are aware of the importance of triangulation, you could develop this initial questionnaire into a series of semi-structured interviews with five of the respondents who completed the questionnaire. You could also do secondary research on the internet to find out about other published accounts that link to your own research. This will help the validity and reliability of your findings. If you also show that all your research participants have had their confidentiality respected, you can also say that you are aware of the importance of ethical principles.

Activity 6.6

When you are in a Lifelong Learning Sector setting, take a research diary and make a note of which aspects of practice could be studied as an example of action research. Think about what you would need to do so that the research was valid and reliable.

We can now complete the chapter by focusing our discussion on critically appraising the research process by thinking about its value for the Lifelong Learning Sector.

Critical appraisal of the research process

The sort of research model that you use and the methods that are applied to your research are, as we have emphasized, determined by the nature of your research question and your research objectives. It is also important to consider the advantages and disadvantages of the different research models and methods.

Appraising normative research

The normative model of research has the advantage of being a large-scale approach to answering the research question. The surveys and experiments that are conducted within this research framework will typically generate much data that can be arranged to present a seemingly formidable answer. Another advantage of this approach to research is the emphasis that is placed on being 'objective' and 'scientific'. Bryman (2004: 11) argues that within this perspective, the research must always be conducted in a way that is 'value free'. A further advantage of the scientific nature of the normative approach is the 'definite' nature of the findings. Through applying statistics, you are able to give a definite answer to your research question. In appraising the value of the normative approach to research, Bryman (2004: 13) argues that a difficulty with this research model rests with the confusion over the difference between the normative perspective and scientific research. In other words, is this model of research the same as 'scientific philosophy' or different? If the research model is different, how does it differ? Bryman also suggests that it is also not clear whether it is appropriate to study 'society' in a scientific way. This is because human beings interact in ways that are often contrary to the scientific model of the world.

The OFSTED inspection process bases many of its findings on normative data. Inspectors visit Lifelong Learning Sector establishments to compare and contrast the data that they gather with the establishment's 'self-evaluation document'. This process is criticised by Lucas (2007) because it contributes to 'standards-driven education'. Lucas argues that 'standards-driven education' (in other words, education that is based on the findings of inspection regimes) has become valued more than 'education' (in the pure sense of the term). The argument runs that it is now more important to please the inspectorate than it is to become an educated person who can think about the world in a different way. It is implied that a consequence of this inspection process is the replacement of educational values with educational statistics. This may be an indirect result of the emphasis that is placed on normative research.

Appraising interpretive research

The interpretive model of research places an emphasis on the 'phenomenology' of human experience. Bryman (2004: 13) summarizes this idea as 'a philosophy that is concerned with the question of how individuals make sense of the world around them and how in particular the philosopher should bracket out preconceptions in his or her grasp of the world'. An advantage of this model of research is the attention that is given to the creativity of the research process. This means that interpretivism argues that researching human beings is an entirely different process to 'scientific research'. As opposed to looking for large-scale general theories, the researcher is looking at small-scale interpretations of social meaning. The advantage of this approach is that it is possible to recognize the profound nature of human interaction. This suggests that a scientific approach, with its emphasis on 'reason' and 'rationality', may miss the creative and inventive nature of human interaction. A difficulty of this model of research is seen in the Geertz (1988: 2) quote that the research process can become akin to 'the lady sawed in half' that is 'done but never really done at all'. As a result of the emphasis that is placed upon 'interpretation', the intensity of the research process can mean that the research findings are so localized and small scale that it is impossible to generate any general theory. This point is reinforced by Bryman (2004: 16) who argues that interpretivist research represents 'tendencies rather than definite points of correspondence'.

If this argument is developed, you can challenge any interpretive research by claiming that the findings are representative of 'views and opinions' but little else. This can mean that it becomes difficult to generate theory from the research findings because of their small-scale, intense, and localized nature.

If the interpretive model of research is accepted within the Lifelong Learning Sector, this may lead to notions of communities of professional practice being accepted as a principle of good practice. A negative consequence can be that it becomes difficult to understand what is happening within the global Lifelong Learning Sector. Diffuse individualized communities of practice may be operating within the same educational sector, but they may operate in distinct ways. The result may be that this makes it difficult to regulate the sector. This would go against the ethos that has been established as a norm by OFSTED. Whether this is good or bad for the Lifelong Learning Sector is a matter for debate and consideration!

Appraising action research

Action research can appear to be a diverse and broad approach to the research process. This is acknowledged by Bryman (2004: 277). This can mean that the researcher becomes a central part of the field of study. The advantage of this characteristic of action research is that it enables the collection of 'rich' data about the chosen topic. Paolo Freire (1970) draws attention to the impact that action research has had on developing educational practice. The cyclical nature of the action research process also means that the research model is not 'linear'. It is opposed to the 'thesis, antithesis, synthesis' model of thought that appears to have influenced the normative and interpretive research models. This means that there is the possibility of constantly comparing research findings as the emphasis is placed on gathering as much data as possible in order to inform future practice. Chambers (1983) draws attention to a difficulty with the action research process as a result of its inherently political nature. The researcher is intimately connected with the research process as a practitioner in the area of research. This can mean that it becomes difficult to gain an impartial view.

Organizations associated with the Lifelong Learning Sector such as the 'IFL' champion the importance of action research by offering 'action research bursaries'. This suggests that action research is an especially important model of research for the Lifelong Learning Sector. It can be argued that involvement with action research is a profound and empowering experience because an opportunity is provided to evaluate and amend professional practice. It can also be suggested that some of the finest academic conferences are based on presentations of action research. This encourages teachers to reflect on professional practice with a view to adapting existing strategies to 'best practice'. This means that action research is extremely useful for teachers in the Lifelong Learning Sector.

Appraising quantitative research

We have said that 'methodology' refers to the model of research that you are using and the data-collection methods that are being applied to answer the research question. Each data-collection method has advantages and disadvantages. Bryman (2004: 62) defines quantitative research as 'entailing the collection of numerical data'. An advantage of having quantitative data is that it can be used to generate statistical findings that appear to offer definite answers to specific research questions. If you read a research report and it states that '80% of UK students aged 14–18 enjoy learning', this appears to be a clear and unambiguous finding. Bryman (2004: 78) does, however, criticize quantitative researchers because 'they fail to distinguish people and social institutions from the world of nature'. This is because the processes that are used in analysing the social world are no different to those that are being used to analyse the natural world. We have already said that human beings have the capacity for inventiveness and creativity. This can mean that a statistical analysis of human behaviour does not account for every aspect of human interaction. This leads Bryman (2004: 78) to propose that quantitative measurement 'possesses an artificial and spurious sense of precision and accuracy'. It can also lead to a somewhat static portrayal of human life as the analysis is structured by statistics. Although it would be wrong to say that quantitative research is 'wrong', these criticisms need to be taken into consideration if you are adopting a quantitative approach to your research question.

We have previously drawn attention to the potential limitations of OFSTED's use of statistics about education. The statistics may appear to have become 'everything'. This can reduce education to 'numbers', and any teacher within the Lifelong Learning Sector knows that education is too profound an experience to be reduced to one variable. The numbers tell only one component of the wider reality. The other components (both positive and negative) need to be acknowledged if an accurate assessment of the Lifelong Learning Sector is to occur.

Appraising qualitative research

Qualitative research is characterized by its focus on non-statistical data. Bryman (2004: 266) defines qualitative research as being 'concerned with words rather than with numbers'. We have said that an advantage of this approach is that it embraces the creativity of the research process. This means that the research process is understood in relation to 'negotiated meanings'. Qualitative research accounts can be detailed, enjoyable accounts that outline the interaction between the researcher and the research subjects. The criticisms of this process are made because of the difficulty that occurs if you want to develop general theory from a small-scale qualitative analysis. Bryman (2004: 284) argues that qualitative research can be 'too subjective'. This can mean that it becomes difficult to replicate a qualitative study because the research process is so particular to the area of study. This in turn means that it is very hard to generalize and give coherent answers to large-scale research questions. The involvement of the researcher within the research process can also mean that it is difficult to see what the researcher actually did and how the conclusions of the research were reached.

Qualitative research accounts of learning and teaching do present the opportunity to reflect on current practice in a creative way. It is often interesting to read the reflections that are made on educational practice. This is exemplified in Ingleby and Hunt's (2008) research on post-compulsory Initial Teacher Training mentoring. The research methodology gathers data via questionnaires and semi-structured interviews. It can be argued that the reflections that are given by students and mentors provide an insight into the mentoring process in an accessible way. This is because the qualitative reflections that are given about mentoring can enable the reader to empathize with the views of the practitioners.

It may also be argued that this research is small scale and localized. This is a potential weakness of the research strategy. Like other examples of qualitative research, this means that it is difficult to make general conclusions about the data that has been gathered. The project may make some interesting small-scale findings about post-compulsory Initial Teacher Training mentoring, but the research cannot be used to make general statements about this aspect of Lifelong Learning.

Summary of key points

This chapter has given an outline of the research process by considering research in relation to the Lifelong Learning Sector. Doing research may not be 'easy', but it is not necessarily a complex challenge. The secret of doing successful research appears to be being prepared. As opposed to doing 'hasty research' it is important to consider which model of research you are going to apply and which research methods you are going to use in order to gather your data. These approaches will be determined by your research question and its associated objectives. The rest of the research process resembles providing the evidence necessary to win an argument. You need to gather enough data to produce an answer that is reliable and valid. For the validity or authenticity of your data to be accepted, you need to make sure that you are aware of the ethics of research. Always ensure that no harm results from your research. If these guidelines are followed, doing research can be one of the most enjoyable aspects of education. It is also one of the most important ways of understanding the Lifelong Learning Sector context. This makes doing research especially relevant to your professional role. Within the chapter, we have referred to Lucas's (2007) phrase 'standards-driven education'. It can be argued that education that is based on research is opposed to this phrase. This is because teaching and learning that is informed by research can represent a synthesis of experience and wisdom. It can also be proposed that these two qualities constitute central aspects of good practice within the Lifelong Learning Sector.

This chapter links to the following SVUK professional standards:

Professional Values

> AS 4: Reflection and evaluation of their own practice and their continuing professional development as teachers.
>
> AS 7: Improving the quality of their practice.

Professional Knowledge and Understanding

> AK 1.1: What motivates learners to learn and the importance of learners' experience and aspirations.
>
> AK 3.1: Issues of equality, diversity and inclusion.
>
> AK 4.1: Principles, frameworks and theories which underpin good practice in learning and teaching.
>
> AK 4.2: The impact of own practice on individuals and their learning.
>
> AK 4.3: Ways to reflect, evaluate and use research to develop own practice and to share good practice with others.
>
> AK 5.1: Ways to communicate and collaborate with colleagues and/or others to enhance learners' experience.

Professional Practice

> AP 4.2: Reflect on and demonstrate commitment to improvement of own personal and teaching skills through regular evaluation and use of feedback.
>
> AP 4.3: Share good practice with others and engage in continuing professional development through reflection, evaluation and appropriate use of research.
>
> AP 7.3: Use feedback to develop own practice within the organization's systems.

Self-assessment questions

> Question 1: What are the names of three research models that are relevant to the Lifelong Learning Sector?
>
> Question 2: How can teachers apply the research process to maximize professional practice within the Lifelong Learning Sector?
>
> Question 3: Give an example of strength and weakness of each of the three research models outlined in this chapter.

Moving on feature

This chapter has introduced you to the research process. Try to think of a research question and research objectives that would link to one of the main chapters in the book.

Further Reading

Bryman, A. (2004), *Social Research Methods*. Oxford: Oxford University Press.

An excellent book giving a detailed account of the research process, but the material is not always directly related to the Lifelong Learning Sector.

References

Bryman, A. and Cramer, D. (1997), *Quantitative Data Analysis: A Guide for Social Scientists*. London: Routledge.

Bryman, A. (2004), *Social Research Methods*. Oxford: Oxford University Press.

Chambers, R. (1983), *Rural Development: Putting the Last First*. London: Longman.

Denzin, N. K. and Lincoln, Y. (2000), *The Handbook of Qualitative Research*. Thousand Oaks, CA: Sage.

Freire, P. (1970), *Pedagogy of the Oppressed*. London: Continuum.

Geertz, C. (1973), *The Interpretation of Cultures: Selected Essays*. New York: Basic Books.

Geertz, C. (1988), *Works and Lives: The Anthropologist as Author*. Stanford, CA: Stanford University Press.

Geertz, C. (1993), *Local Knowledge: Further Essays in Interpretive Anthropology*. London: Fontana Press.

Gillham, B. (2000), *Case Study Research Methods*. London: Continuum.

Ingleby, E. and Hunt, J. (2008) 'The CPD needs of mentors in post-compulsory Initial Teacher Training in England', *Journal of In-Service Education*, 34, 61–75.

Kreuger, R. (1994), *Moderating Focus Groups*. Thousand Oaks CA: Sage.

Lieberman, J. (2009). 'Reinventing teacher professional norms and identities: the role of lesson study and learning communities', *Professional Development in Education*, 35, 83–99.

Lucas, N. (2007), 'The in-service training of adult literacy, numeracy and English for speakers of other languages teachers in England; the challenges of a 'standards-led model', *Journal of In-Service Education*, 33, 125–142.

Online dictionary. Online: (www.dictionary.reference.com).

Opie, L. (2004), *Doing Educational Research: A Guide to First Time Researchers*. London: Sage.

Reece, I. and Walker, S. (2007), *Teaching Training and Learning: A Practical Guide*. Sunderland: Business Education Publishers.

Wenger, E. (1998), *Communities of Practice: Learning Meaning and Identity*. Cambridge: Cambridge University Press.

Conclusion

This book is concerned with teaching and learning in the Lifelong Learning Sector. We have seen that the sector is characterized by diversity. There are many different educational institutions. These institutions can offer a huge range of educational programmes. This can mean that teaching in the Lifelong Learning Sector can represent a fascinating challenge. It can also mean that becoming a teacher in this educational context requires constant reflection on professional practice. This is a theme characterizing the work of Race (2006) and Petty (2009). In Chapter 5, we recommended that it is important to be as flexible as possible in order to meet the challenges of teaching in the Lifelong Learning Sector. This is because it can be hard to be a perfectionist if you are working within this educational environment. It is unrealistic to expect perfect teaching rooms, perfect funding and perfectly behaved learners and colleagues! The reality can be altogether different. This means that it is important to make the best of your circumstances by reflecting on what works and what is likely to produce negative learning experiences. As we have already seen, anyone teaching in the Lifelong Learning Sector needs to learn how to teach. We have also suggested that the teaching process is based on learning, experience and reflective practice. It is these fascinating processes that characterize the Lifelong Learning Sector. This means that this educational context can both challenge and inspire teachers and learners.

The Lifelong Learning Sector is often associated with change. Curriculum change may combine with changes of learners and staff. Since 2002, there have also been changes to teaching accommodation as a result of the FE rebuilding programme. In view of this changing learning environment, it is important to review teaching and learning strategies. It is difficult to rely on the same teaching notes as the Lifelong Learning Sector can be mercurial and 'fast-moving'. It is equally important to be open to new ideas in respect of changing teaching strategies. My own realization of this point occurred upon learning about 'learning preferences'. I adapted my formative assessment activities by considering the learning strengths of my students. I found that this strategy engaged my students with the learning process. Students who had previously studied within a formal learning context appeared to be filled with enthusiasm about the curriculum. This change in my teaching practice was a consequence of reflecting upon teaching and learning. It led to my development as a teacher. The experience also enhanced my understanding of the nature of the Lifelong Learning Sector. It increased my awareness of the challenges and rewards of working within this diverse educational sector.

Chapter content

In this book, the six main chapters have been written upon considering the academic modules that contribute to Teesside University's QTLS PGCE. These modules have been written by considering the standards for QTLS. We have seen that the book is a practical text for anyone teaching in the Lifelong Learning Sector. The book's formative activities consider a number of learning and teaching themes by reflecting on pedagogy and andragogy. The aim of these activities has been to encourage reflective practice within the Lifelong Learning Sector.

We have also tried to emphasize the importance of the link between theory, practice, reflection and learning about teaching. In other words, the theoretical concepts have been considered as being most useful when they are applied to the educational contexts of the Lifelong Learning Sector. All of book's chapters have included formative activities that consider teaching and learning within the Lifelong Learning Sector. These activities encourage you to think about the idea that learning about teaching in this educational context is not a static process.

The book's chapters have focused upon six main learning themes:

- Preparing to teach in the Lifelong Learning Sector
- Teaching in the Learning and Skills Sector
- Theories and principles for planning and enabling learning and assessment
- Classroom management
- Curriculum development for inclusive practice
- Research methods for the Lifelong Learning Sector

In Chapter 1, we considered a number of 'preservice' issues that characterize teaching in the Lifelong Learning Sector. The chapter gave an introduction to teaching and learning within the Lifelong Learning Sector by considering some of the basics of planning and preparation for teaching and learning. The chapter also considered a number of key 'pre-service' themes, such as 'lesson planning' and 'resource design', in relation to preparing to teach in the Lifelong Learning Sector.

In Chapter 2, we explored teaching and learning within a variety of educational contexts. The chapter provided an introduction to the key Lifelong Learning theme of 'personal action planning'. The chapter also identified and appraised a number of theories about teaching and learning (such as behaviourism, humanism and constructivism). This content was linked to some central themes in the Lifelong Learning Sector, such as 'forms of assessment' and 'reflective practice'. The chapter content developed the theme that the Lifelong Learning Sector is characterized by a variety of learners. These learners have particular learning needs, so this means that it is important to consider a range of teaching and learning strategies.

In Chapter 3, we considered some of the theories and principles that are important for teaching in respect of planning and enabling learning and assessment. The chapter has reviewed a number of theories and principles of learning, assessment and communication. The chapter has explored how these theories and principles can be used to enable inclusive learning. The final section of the chapter has given a discussion of how teaching and assessment may be developed by applying 'theories of learning' to 'reflection on practice'.

Chapter 4 has applied a number of key psychological perspectives to teaching in the Lifelong Learning Sector. Some of the ideas within behaviourism, humanism, biological, psychodynamic and cognitive theory have been applied to 'classroom management'. These perspectives have been linked to classroom management via case-study examples and formative activities that reinforce learning. At the end of the chapter, there is an assessment of the merits of each of the perspectives in respect of the contribution being made to classroom management.

In Chapter 5, we considered the different educational contexts of the Lifelong Learning Sector. The chapter reflected on 'inclusive practice' by exploring this theme in relation to planning, implementing and evaluating programmes of learning. The chapter considered issues associated with 'inclusion' by addressing a number of key issues that are associated with planning, designing, implementing and reviewing a curriculum that promotes 'inclusive practice'.

Chapter 6 has explored some of the key research perspectives and key research methods that are applied to the Lifelong Learning Sector. The chapter has considered the nature of the research process by identifying and appraising key research paradigms, such as normative, interpretive and action research perspectives. The chapter has explored some of the methodological strategies employed by qualitative and quantitative research on the Lifelong Learning Sector. The chapter included a reflection on the value of these research paradigms and methods by considering the merits of the research process for the Lifelong Learning Sector.

The book has provided a thorough consideration of a number of key themes that impact on the Lifelong Learning Sector. As opposed to being a general teacher education textbook, this material has been specifically written for the Lifelong Learning teacher education programmes based on the QTLS standards. This allows the content to be based on practical experience and sound academic analysis.

Formative learning

The book has strived to enable learning via a number of interactive activities within each chapter. Alongside these activities, each chapter is supported by case studies and research tasks. Moreover, the book facilitates the development of analytical skills by reflecting on the academic content. This means that alongside the interactive learning activities there are key references so that learning to teach in the Lifelong Learning Sector can be synthesized in relation to these texts.

The QTLS standards

Since 2005, the curriculum of the Lifelong Learning Sector has been influenced by LLUK. LLUK can be regarded as having a responsibility for the professional development of the Lifelong Learning Sector. We have also seen that the subsidiary organization SVUK operates alongside LLUK and is responsible for approving and endorsing teacher training qualifications within the post-compulsory sector. This means that the responsibilities of the Further Education Teaching Organisation (FENTO) are now the concern of LLUK and SVUK. This change to the sector has also witnessed the DFES introducing a new curriculum for teacher training in the post-16 sector. The consequence of this change has been the introduction of a new set of occupational standards in 2007. Each of the main chapters has referred to the new standards in order to emphasize the importance of the sector responding to a broad lifelong learning agenda. Whereas the previous FENTO standards were considered to be 'limited' due to their focus on 'further education', the new emphasis that is placed on 'lifelong learning' is deemed as being more relevant to the variety of learning and teaching that characterizes the diverse post-compulsory curriculum. The new standards are ideally considered to be detailed and comprehensive.

The price of standards-driven education

The introduction of the new occupational standards can have indirect consequences for the Lifelong Learning Sector. It can mean that an emphasis is placed upon educational standards to the detriment of the educational process. The phrase 'robbing Peter to pay Paul' may be used as analogy for this occurrence. According to Rogers (1985), this phrase originates with the work of John Wycliffe in 1380. What appears to have happened in the Lifelong Learning

Sector is that a 'standards-driven' educational agenda now exists alongside other educational values within the same educational context. A number of authors, such as Coffield (2004), Hale (2008), Lieberman (2009), Lucas (2007), and Wenger (1998), have commented on the difference that exists between standards-driven education and education that establishes 'communities of professional practice'. In other words, there is a debate about the purpose of education. The question at the centre of this debate asks whether education exists for the sake of standards or whether it is a means of enlightening individuals? All of the previously cited authors discuss the consequences of standards-driven education. It can be argued that if too much of an emphasis is placed on educational standards, the educational process may become distorted. This can be seen with a number of Lifelong Learning educational initiatives.

An interesting area to consider in respect of this issue is mentoring. The work of Ingleby and Hunt (2008) appears to indicate that mentors within the Lifelong Learning context struggle to gain professional acceptance. Alongside struggling to achieve professional recognition, Lifelong Learning Sector mentors may not use the same 'way of talking' about teaching as their mentees. This research concludes that the current nature of Lifelong Learning Sector mentoring is a fascinating consequence of the standards-driven educational agenda.

In his poem 'The Road Not Taken', Robert Frost (2001) writes,

> Two roads diverged in a wood, and I,
> I took the one less travelled by,
> And that has made all the difference. (155)

The sentiments in these lines link to an interpretation of education that focuses on a literal translation of the word. The Latin verb 'educere' (with its implication of individuals coming to a new and different appreciation of the world) draws attention to the role that education can have in developing individual potential. As stated previously, this interpretation of education is discussed by Coffield (2004), Hale (2008), Lieberman (2009), Lucas (2007) and Wenger (1998). Education for enlightenment is juxtaposed to standards-driven education. The argument is developed to give a critique of educational initiatives that appear to have political or economic motives.

This argument can also be related to the Geertzian (1995: 120) critique of fieldwork. Geertz argues that many fieldwork accounts within social science may miss the crucial element of the fieldwork experience through being overly concerned about presenting their findings to meet the established norms of academic 'social science'. The argument runs that research and publishing protocol can mean that 'experience' is not accurately relayed. This means that the encounter may become different as it is made to fit the agenda of academic publishing houses. This analogy can also be applied to the Lifelong Learning Sector. In other words, if this educational context did exist for pure educational motives, this may help in engendering the sentiments that Frost celebrates. The standards-driven nature of sector can mean, however, that the educational experience may be less than pure.

The ironic aspect of the above argument is that despite the attention that has been given to the Lifelong Learning Sector in recent years, the standards-driven nature of the context appears to contribute to producing an uncertain educational environment. This may be because the emphasis is placed on meeting standards as opposed to being there for educational reasons alone.

The reality of the Lifelong Learning Sector appears to be that whether full-time or part-time, teachers and learners can experience a challenging experience of teaching, learning and assessment in meeting programme targets. The intensity of the process can mean that both teachers and learners may be unable to reflect fully on their developmental journey within the Lifelong Learning Sector. Brookes (2005: 45) argues that this occurrence is a result of the lack of a 'systematic monitoring of the training process'. This argument can be developed to propose that if the Lifelong Learning Sector was less concerned with occupational standards a more complete educational experience may result. This might help teachers and learners to reflect on their educational journey.

There appears to be much current discussion about this issue within the Lifelong Learning Sector. For example, one of the themes of a conference organized by the Universities for the Education of Teachers (UCET) in November 2008 was the debate over the effectiveness or otherwise of standards-driven education. The current interest in this issue can imply that 'reflective practice' is a recent development when in fact it has a long history. Ingleby and Hunt (2008: 62) use the work of Brookes (2005: 43) to support this argument. As far back as 1805, Bell and Lancaster recommended that new teachers needed to be inducted into the profession by 'taking a share in the office of tuition' as opposed to having theoretical training in pedagogy (Brookes, 2005: 44). In other words, it was recommended that reflective practice could help in developing individual teachers. The characteristic idea behind this process is that reflecting on professional practice is a crucial part of the teaching process.

Ingleby and Hunt (2008: 62) acknowledge that 200 years later, the English inspection agency OFSTED have commented in numerous Lifelong Learning Sector inspections that this process of developing reflective practice is underdeveloped. It can be argued that if less emphasis was placed on educational standards, more emphasis could be given to reflective practice.

Reflective practice

In contrast to emphasising the importance of educational standards, a major aim of the PGCE programme at the Teesside University is to nurture professionals who are able to reflect on aspects of best practice. The authors argue that this book facilitates self-analysis in relation to the Lifelong Learning Sector. This enables the possibility of development in meeting the complex needs of teachers and learners working in the sector. Ideally, the sector will move more in the direction of reflective practice and less in the direction of standards-driven education.

References

Brookes, W. (2005), 'The graduate teacher programme in England: mentor training, quality assurance and the findings of inspection'. *Journal of In-Service Education*, 31, 43-61.

Coffield, F. (2004), *Learning Styles*. London: LSDA Publications.

Frost, R. (2001), *The Poetry of Robert Frost*. Colchester: Vintage.

Geertz, C. (1995), *After the Fact: Two Countries, Four Decades, One Anthropologist*. Cambridge, MA: Harvard University Press.

Hale, J. A. (2008), *A Guide to Curriculum Planning*. Thousand Oaks, CA: Corwin Press.

Ingleby, E. and Hunt, J. (2008), 'The CPD needs of mentors in post-compulsory initial teacher training in England'. *Journal of In-Service Education*, 34, 61-74.

Lieberman, J. (2009), 'Reinventing teacher professional norms and identities: the role of lesson study and learning communities'. *Professional Development in Education*, 35, 83-99.

Lucas, N. (2007), 'The in-service training of adult literacy, numeracy and English for speakers of other languages teachers in England; the challenges of a "standards-led model"'. *Journal of In-Service Education*, 33, 125-142.

Petty, G. (2004), *Teaching Today: A Practical Guide*. London: Nelson Thornes.

— (2009), *Teaching Today: A Practical Guide*. London: Nelson Thornes.

Race, P. (2002), *The Lecturer's Toolkit*. London: Routledge.

— (2006), *The Lecturer's Toolkit*. London: Routledge.

Rogers, J. (1985), *The Dictionary of Clichés*. New York: Ballantine Books.

Wenger, E. (1998), *Communities of Practice: Learning, Meaning and Identity*. Cambridge, Cambridge University Press.

Answers to Self-Assessment Questions

Chapter 1

Answer 1

Excellent planning and preparation skills
Is interested in their learners and takes time to get to know them and what they are interested in
A good motivator
Is interesting
Sound subject knowledge
Links theory to practice using examples and activities
Offers opportunities for teacher assessment and learner self-assessment
Can differentiate and offer challenge

Answer 2

Teacher aim and learning outcomes clearly shown
Shows a range of teaching and learning activities
Clear timings linked to activities and assessment
Activities and assessment ensures achievement of learning outcomes
Clear preamble and content section
Space made available for self-evaluation following the session

Answer 3

Self-assessment using a questionnaire
Asking learners for feedback
Using a model of reflection

Chapter 2

Answer 1

Discovery learning
Research

Group activities
Role play
Simulation/games

Answer 2

Can work alone or in small groups, on and off campus

Have access to range of learning resources other than the tutor

Can take exams at own convenience

Can enrol at flexible times of the year

Take ownership of their learning, become reflective learners and be empowered

Are more motivated and committed towards learning because they become partners in the learning process

Can work and learn in partnership

Answer 3

Be clear and direct, whereby the reasons for assessment decisions are fully explained in language which is direct and unambiguous rather than vague or 'beating around the bush'

Constructive, because it is important to offer advice for further action which is in the student's capacity to take

Descriptive of what the tutor has seen/observed/thinks rather than over-evaluative or judgemental

Helpful and supportive on the tutor's part (this attitude must be fully communicated to the student)

Well timed, being given as soon as is practicable after evidence has been demonstrated and at a time when the student is receptive to feedback

Fully understood by the student, with the tutor making every effort to ensure this, leaving no unresolved questions, misunderstandings or conclusions

Specific, being related to particular incidents or learning events

Chapter 3

1. Learning is a relatively permanent change in behaviour.
2. Advertising works by association. In other words, associating a stimulus with a positive response. This means that if you go to this country on holiday the weather will be great, you'll experience fabulous beaches and so on.
3. Various – according to the individual (for example, when I go to my diet club and I lose half a stone, I am rewarded with a silver tick!).
4. Behaviourists believe that all behaviour is learnt.
5. A major cognitive theorist is Gestalt/Piaget.
6. Carl Rogers, Abraham Maslow and Malcolm Knowles.
7. Surface learning can be described as shallow or superficial as it is simply the recalling of factual information.
8. Teaching by asking (instead of teaching by telling), ask higher order questions (Bloom's taxonomy), use case studies.

Chapter 4

Answer 1

The five major schools of psychology are: psychoanalytical, behaviourist, humanistic, neuro-biological and cognitive.

Answer 2

The best way of applying psychology to classroom management is through holistic therapies that combine the principles of behaviourism, humanism, cognitive, psychodynamic and neurobiological psychology to meeting the complex needs of individuals.

Answer 3: Answers to Chapter 4 self-assessment questions

School of thought	Strength	Weakness
Behaviourism	Acknowledgement of environmental influences on the mind. This can be especially useful for classroom management as the importance of managing the physical learning environment is regarded as being a critical part of the learning process	A tendency to neglect individual creativity. In other words, there is such an emphasis placed on the importance of the surrounding environment that the ability of individuals to influence the learning environment may be under emphasized
Humanism	Acknowledgement of how individuals manipulate external variables. This theory can be applied to classroom management by emphasizing the importance of being aware that each learner is a unique individual. An example of where this can be seen is through the development of 'ILPs'. It may be argued that these documents hold the potential to put Rogerian theory into practice, as long as they are used for this intention as opposed to meeting the requirements of what Lucas (2007) refers to as 'standards driven education'. Lucas uses this phrase to criticize education that meets the requirements of the inspectorate, but does not necessarily meet the needs of learners	Rogerian theory is idealistic. At the centre of the theory is the proposal that individuals are 'innately good'. This may be argued as being an 'ideal' as opposed to being 'reality'. The theory does not provide a satisfactory answer for dealing with learners who have a completely different set of values to those of their teacher except for identifying that a 'would should' dilemma is likely to characterize the relationship
Psychodynamic	Acknowledgement of the workings of the unconscious mind. This theory may be useful for learners who are unable to be part of the conventional learning environment for complex psychological reasons. These learners may be helped through psychodynamic counselling. This counselling may help in alleviating profound psychological problems that are located within the workings of the unconscious mind	The theory is not methodologically proven. This can mean that psychodynamic therapies work through 'good fortune' as opposed to 'science'. This means that the therapies may be unreliable

(Continued)

| Cognitive | Acknowledgement of the different thought proc- esses during human cognitive development. This helps to raise awareness of the importance of using learning and teaching methods that are appropriate to the needs of the learners. Vygotsky's 'social learning' can also be used to justify the importance of using group work as a teaching and learning method that can enhance classroom management | The idea of stages of development is not necessarily the case. Cognitive development may be more of a process than a series of stages. This means that it is important to treat learners as individuals as opposed to viewing them as a collective whole |
| Neurobiological | Acknowledgement of the link between human thoughts and hormones/chromosomes. There are learners (for example, learners with Attention Deficit Hyperactivity Disorder) who may find that their ability to cope with classroom learning is helped with medication | The theory is biologically reductionist. It is not always known which medication works with which learners and why the medication works |

Chapter 5

Answer 1

Inclusive practice is the use of a variety of differentiated approaches to teaching in the class-room. This is in order to deliver the curricula content in such a way as to promote access to learning for as many learners as possible.

Answer 2

Course content and overall aims of the course
Time constraints
The content of the curriculum to be delivered and the appropriate order of delivery
The teaching and learning strategies and the type of knowledge and skills to be developed
Any requirements of professional bodies/occupational standards
Assessment of learning
Specialist knowledge input
The available physical and human resources
Specific detail about learners' entry behaviour and the individual needs of each learner
Learning styles
Abilities of the learners
Equality and diversity issues

Answer 3

1. Your view of the situation, as the delivering practitioner
2. The learner's view
3. Other practitioners views (colleagues/learning mentor)
4. The views of established theory

Chapter 6

Answer 1

The three research models that are especially relevant to the Lifelong Learning Sector are the normative, interpretive and action research perspectives.

Answer 2

The best way of applying the research process to the Lifelong Learning Sector is through identifying a possible topic of 'action research' so that the research can be used to inform future professional practice. In the earlier part of this chapter, we exemplified 'learning p references' as a possible action research project. If you selected a cohort of 25 learners as the research sample, it would be possible to administer a questionnaire to these learners to identify their perceptions of the effectiveness of learning preferences. This initial questionnaire data could then form the basis for a series of six semi-structured interviews in order to develop the research themes that have appeared within the questionnaire data. Other published research on learning preferences could be used as secondary data to support the primary research findings. The data could be analysed using the Geertzian notion of 'thick description' in order to identify the main research themes. The research findings could then be summarized and presented to colleagues within the Lifelong Learning Sector. This research project would then become a way of having 'research-informed teaching'. The project becomes a means of contributing to the body of knowledge that informs educational practice within the Lifelong Learning Sector. It can be argued that this becomes a way of maximizing professional practice within the Lifelong Learning Sector.

Answer 3: Answers to Chapter 6 self-assessment questions

Research model	Strength	Weakness
Normative	Acknowledgement of quantitative data	A tendency to neglect individuals creating social meaning. We argued that this is a potential negative consequence of the OFSTED inspection process
Interpretive	Acknowledgement of how individuals negotiate meaning	Research is usually small scale and localized. We argued that this means that it is difficult to establish general impressions of the Lifelong Learning Sector
Action research	The research can be used to inform future professional practice	It is difficult to be 'impartial' as an action researcher as you are intimately involved with the research process

Index

Note: Page numbers in **bold** denote figures and tables.